The Balancing Act

Language, Speech, and Communication

The Balancing Act

Combining Symbolic
and Statistical Approaches
to Language

edited by Judith L. Klavans
and Philip Resnik

The MIT Press
Cambridge, Massachusetts
London, England

This book was set in Times Roman by Omegatype Typography, Inc. and was printed and bound in the United States of America.

Library of Congress Cataloging-in-Publication Data

The balancing act : combining symbolic and statistical approaches to
    language / edited by Judith L. Klavans and Philip Resnik.
        p.   cm. — (Language, speech, and communication)
    Selected papers, rev., of a workshop held at the 32nd Annual
    Meeting of the Association for Computational Linguistics, at New
    Mexico State University in Las Cruces, N.M., on July 1, 1994.
    Includes bibliographical references and index.
    ISBN 0-262-11218-3 (hc : alk. paper). — ISBN 0-262-61122-8 (pb :
    alk. paper)
    1. Computational linguistics—Congresses. 2. Linguistics—
Statistical methods—Congresses. I. Klavans, Judith L.
II. Resnik, Philip. III. Association for Computational Linguistics.
IV. Series.
P98.5.S83B35   1996
410'.72—dc20   96-2340
                                                         CIP

Contents

Chapter 7

Lance A. Ramshaw
and Mitchell P. Marcus

Chapter 8

Carolyn Penstein Rosé
and Alex H. Waibel

Preface

The chapters in this book come out of a workshop held at the 32nd Annual Meeting of the Association for Computational Linguistics, at New Mexico State University in Las Cruces, New Mexico, on 1 July 1994. The purpose of the workshop was to provide a forum in which to explore combined symbolic and statistical approaches in computational linguistics.

To many researchers, the mere notion of combining approaches to the study of language seems anathema. Indeed, in the past it has appeared necessary to choose between two radically different research agendas, studying two essentially different kinds of data. On the one hand, we find cognitively motivated theories of language in the tradition of generative linguistics, with introspective data as primary evidence. On the other, we find approaches motivated by empirical coverage, with collections of naturally occurring data as primary evidence. Each approach has its own kinds of theory, methodology, and criteria for success.

Although underlying philosophical differences go back much further, the genesis of generative grammar in the late 1950s and early 1960s drew attention to the issues of concern in this book. At that time, there was a thriving quantitative linguistics community, in both the United States and Europe, that had originated following World War II in the surge of development of sophisticated quantitative approaches to scientific problems [Shannon and Weaver, 1949]. These quantitative approaches were built on the foundation of observable data as the primary source of evidence. The appearance of generative grammar [Chomsky, 1957], with its emphasis on intuitive grammaticality judgments, led to confrontation with the existing quantitative approach, and the rift between the two communities, arising from firmly held opinions on both sides, prevented productive interaction. Computational approaches to language grew up during this feud, with much of computational linguistics dominated by the theoretical perspective of generative grammar, hostile to quantitative methods, and much of the speech community dominated by statistical information theory, hostile to theoretical linguistics.

Although a few natural language processing (NLP) groups persisted in taking a probabilistic approach in the 1970s and 1980s, the rule-governed, theory-driven approach dominated the field, even among the many industrial teams working on NLP (e.g. [Woods and Kaplan, 1971; Petrick, 1971; Grosz, 1983]). The influence of the linguists' generative revolution on NLP projects was overwhelming. Statistical or even simply quantitative notions survived in this environment only as secondary considerations, included for the purpose of optimization but rarely thought of as an integral part of a system's core design. At the same time, speech processing grew more mature, building on an information-theoretic tradition that emphasized the induction of statistical models from training data (e.g. [Bahl et al., 1983; Flanagan, 1972]).

For quite some time, the two communities continued with little to say to each other. However, in the late 1980s and early 1990s, the field of NLP underwent a radical shift. Fueled partly by the agenda of the Defense Advanced Research Projects Agency (DARPA), a major source of American funding for both speech and natural language processing, and partly by the dramatic increase world wide in the availability of electronic texts, the two communities found themselves in close contact. The result for computational linguists was that long-standing problems in their domain—for example, identifying the syntactic category of the words in a sentence, or resolving prepositional phrase ambiguity in parsing—were tackled using the same sorts of statistical methods prevalent in speech recognition, often with some success. The specific techniques varied, but all were founded upon the idea of inducing the knowledge necessary to solve a problem by statistically analyzing large corpora of naturally occurring text, rather than building in such knowledge in the form of symbolic rules.

Initially, the interest in corpus-based statistical methods rekindled all the old controversies—rationalist vs. empiricist philosophies, theory-driven vs. data-driven methodologies, symbolic vs. statistical techniques (e.g., see discussion in [Church and Mercer, 1993]). The Balancing Act workshop we held in 1994 was planned when the rhetoric was at its height, at a time when it seemed to us that, even if some people were working on common ground, not enough people were talking about it. The field of computational linguistics is now settling down somewhat: for the most part, researchers have become less unwaveringly adversarial over ideological questions, and have instead begun to focus on the search for a coherent combination of approaches.

Why have things changed? First, there is an increasing realization, within each community, that achieving core goals may require expertise possessed by the other. Quantitative approaches add robustness and coverage to traditionally brittle and narrow symbolic natural language systems, permitting, for example, the automated or semiautomated acquisition of lexical knowledge (e.g., terminology, names, translation equivalents). At the same time, quantitative approaches are critically dependent on underlying assumptions about the nature of the data, and more people are concluding that pushing applications to the next level of performance will require quantitative models that are linguistically better informed; inductive statistical methods perform better in the face of limited data when they are biased with accurate prior knowledge.

A second source of change is the critical computational resources not widely available when quantitative methods were last in vogue. Fast computers, cheap disk space, CD-ROMs for distributing data, and funded data-collection initiatives have become the rule rather than the exception. The Brown Corpus of American English, Francis and Kučera's landmark project of the 1960s [Kučera and Francis, 1967], now has companions that are larger, that are annotated in more linguistic detail, and that consist of data from multiple languages (e.g. [LDC, 1996; ICAME, 1996]).

Third, there is a general push toward applications that work with language in a broad, real-world context, rather than within the narrow domains of traditional symbolic NLP systems. With the advent of such broad coverage applications, language technology is positioned to help satisfy some real demands in the marketplace: large-vocabulary speech recognition has become a daily part of life for many people unable to use a computer keyboard [Wilpon, 1994], rough automatic translation of unrestricted text is finding its way into on-line services, and locating full text information on the World Wide Web has become a priority [Foley and Pitkow, 1994]. Applications of this kind are faced with unpredictable input from users who are unfamiliar with the technology and its limitations, which makes their tasks harder; on the other hand, users are adjusting to less than perfect results. All these considerations—coverage, robustness, acceptability of graded performance—call out for systems that take advantage of large-scale quantitative methods.

Finally, the resurgence of interest in methods grounded in empiricism is partly the result of an intellectual pendulum swinging back in that direction. Thus, even independent of applications, we see more of a focus, on the scientific side of computational linguistics, on the properties of naturally occurring data, the objective and quantitative evaluation of hypotheses against such data, and the construction of models that explicitly take variability and uncertainty into account. Developments of this kind also have parallels in related areas such as sociolinguistics [Sankoff, 1978] and psycholinguistics; in the latter field, for example, probabilistic models of on-line sentence processing treat frequency effects, and more generally, weighted probabilistic interactions, as fundamental to the description of on-line performance, in much the same way that empiricists see the probabilistic nature of language as fundamental to its description (e.g. [Tabossi et al., 1992]; also see [Ferstl, 1993]). This book focuses on the trend toward empirical methods as it bears on the engineering side of NLP, but we believe that trend will also continue to have important implications for the study of language as a whole.

The premise of this book is that there is no necessity for a polar division. Indeed, one of our goals in this book is to change that perception. We hold that there is in fact no contradiction of defection involved in combining approaches. Rather, combining "symbolic" and "statistical" approaches to language is a kind of balancing act in which the symbolic and the statistical are properly thought of as parts, both essential, of a unified whole.

The complementary nature of the contribution of these seemingly discrepant approaches is not as contradictory as it seems. An obvious fact that is often forgotten is that every use of statistics is based upon a symbolic model. No matter what the application, statistics are founded upon an underlying probability model, and that model is, at its core, symbolic and algebraic rather than continuous and quantitative. For language, in particular, the natural units of manipulation in any statistical model are discrete constructs such as phoneme, morpheme, word, and so forth, as well as discrete relationships among these constructs such as surface adjacency or predicate-argument relationships. Regardless of the details of the model, the numerical probabilities are simply meaningless except in the context of the model's symbolic underpinnings. On this view, there is no such things as a "purely statistical" method. Even hidden Markov models, the exemplar of statistical methods inherited from the speech community, are based upon an algebraic description of language that amounts to an assumption of finite-state generative capacity. Conversely, symbolic underpinnings alone are not enough to capture the variability inherent in naturally occurring linguistic data, its resistance to inflexible, terse characterizations. In short, the essence of the balancing act can be found in the opening chapters of any elementary text on probability theory: the core, symbolic underpinnings of a probability model reflect those constraints and assumptions that must be built in, and form the basis for a quantitative side that reflects uncertainty, variability, and gradedness of preferences.

The aim of this book is to explore the balancing act that must take place when symbolic and statistical approaches are brought together—it contains foreshadowings of powerful partnerships in the making between the more linguistically motivated approaches within the tradition of generative grammar and the more empirically driven approaches from the tradition of information theory. Research of this kind requires basic choices: What knowledge will be represented symbolically and how will it be obtained? What assumptions underlie the statistical model? What principles motivate the symbolic model? What is the researcher gaining by combining approaches? These questions, and the metaphor of the balancing act, provide a unifying theme to the contributions in this volume.

References

L. R. Bahl, F. Jelinek, and R. L. Mercer. 1983. A maximum likelihood approach to continuous speech recognition. *IEEE Transactions on Pattern Analysis and Machine Intelligence,* PAMI-5:179–190.

Noam Chomsky. 1957. *Syntactic Structures.* The Hague, Mouton.

Kenneth W. Church and Robert Mercer. 1993. Introduction to the special on computational linguistics using large corpora. *Computational Linguistics,* 19(1):1–24.

James L. Flanagan. 1972. *Speech analysis, synthesis and perception,* 2nd edition. New York, Springer-Verlag.

Evelyn Ferstl. 1993. The role of lexical information and discourse context in syntactic processing: a review of psycholinguistic studies. Cognitive Science Technical Report 93-03, University of Colorado at Boulder.

Jim Foley and James Pitkow, editors. 1994. *Research Priorities for the World-Wide Web: Report of the NSF workshop sponsored by the Information, Robotics, and Intelligent Systems Division.* National Science Foundation, October 1994.

Barbara Grosz. TEAM: a transportable natural language interface system. In *Proceedings of the Conference on Applied Natural Language Processing.* Association for Computational Linguistics, Morristown, N.J., February 1983.

ICAME. ICAME corpus collection. World Wide Web page, 1996. http://nora.hd.uib.no/corpora.html.

H. Kučera and W. Francis. 1967. *Computational Analysis of Present-Day American English.* Providence, R.I., Brown University Press.

LDC. Linguistic Data Consortium (LDC) home page. World Wide Web page, June 1996. http://www.cis.upenn.edu/~ldc/.

Stanley R. Petrick. 1971. Transformational analysis. In Randall Rustin, editor, *Natural Language Processing.* New York, Algorithmics Press.

David Sankoff. 1978. Linguistic variation: Models and methods. New York, Academic Press.

Claude E. Shannon and Warren Weaver. 1949. *The Mathematical Theory of Communication.* Urbana, University of Illinois Press.

Patrizia Tabossi, Michael Spivey-Knowlton, Ken McRae, and Michael Tanenhaus. 1992. Semantic effects on syntactic ambiguity resolution: evidence for a constraint-based resolution process. *Attention and Performance,* 15: 598–615.

Jay G. Wilpon. 1994. Applications of Voice-Processing Technology in Telecommunications. In David B. Roe and Jay G. Wilpon, editors, *Voice Communications Between Humans and Machines.* Washington, D.C., National Academy of Sciences, National Academy Press.

W. A. Woods and R. Kaplan. 1971. The lunar sciences natural language information system. Technical Report 2265. Cambridge, Mass., Bolt, Beranek, and Newman.

Acknowledgments

Since time is the one immaterial object which we cannot influence—neither speed up nor slow down, add to nor diminish—it is an imponderably valuable gift.
—Maya Angelou, *Wouldn't Take Nothing for My Journey Now*

Many people have given of their time in the preparation of this book, from its first stages as a workshop to its final stages of publication. The first set of people to thank are those who submitted papers to the original workshop. We had an overwhelming number of very high-quality papers submitted, and regretted not being able to run a longer workshop on the topic. The issue of combining approaches is clearly part of the research agenda of many computational linguists, as demonstrated by these submissions. Those authors who have chapters in this book have revised them several times in response to two rounds of reviews, and we are grateful to them for their efforts. Our anonymous reviewers for these chapters gave generously of their time—each article was reviewed several times, and each reviewer did a careful and thorough job—and although they are anonymous to the outside world, their generosity is known to themselves, and we thank them quietly. We also deeply acknowledge the time Amy Pierce of The MIT Press gave to us at many stages along the way. Her vision and insight have been a gift, and she has contributed to ensuring the excellent quality of the final set of chapters in the book.

We are grateful to the Association for Computational Linguistics (ACL) for its support and supportiveness, especially its financial commitment to the Balancing Act workshop—and doubly pleased that the attendance at the workshop helped us give something tangible back to the organization. The ACL 1994 conference and post-conference workshops were held at New Mexico State University, with local arrangements handled efficiently and graciously by Janyce Wiebe; we thank her for her time and generosity of spirit. We would also like to thank Sun Microsystems Laboratories for its supportiveness throughout the process of organizing the workshop and putting together this book, especially Cookie Callahan of Sun Labs. Finally, we thank Richard Sproat and Evelyne Tzoukermann for their valuable discussions.

We have enjoyed the experience of working on this topic, since the challenge of combining ways of looking at the world intrigued each of us independently before we joined forces to run the workshop and subsequently edit this book. One of us has training in theoretical linguistics, and has slowly been converted to an understanding of the role of performance data even in linguistic theory. The other had formal education in computer science, with healthy doses of linguistics and psychology, and so arrived in the field with both points of view. We are finding that more and more of our colleagues are coming to believe that maintaining a balance among several approaches to language analysis and understanding is an act worth pursuing.

The Balancing Act

Chapter 1

Statistical Methods and Linguistics

Steven Abney

In general, the view of the linguist toward the use of statistical methods was shaped by the division that took place in the late 1950s and early 1960s between the language engineering community (e.g. [Yngve, 1954]) and the linguistics community (e.g. [Chomsky, 1964]). When Chomsky outlined the three levels of adequacy—observational, descriptive, and explanatory—much of what was in progress in the computational community of the time was labeled as either observational or descriptive with relatively little or no impact on the goal of producing an explanatorily adequate theory of language. The computational linguist was said to deal just with performance, *while the goal of linguistics is to understand* competence. *This point of view was highly influential then and persists to this day as a set of a priori assumptions about the nature of computational work on language.*

Abney's chapter revisits and challenges these assumptions, with the goal of illustrating to the linguist what the rationale might be for the computational linguist in pursuing statistical analyses. He reviews several key areas of linguistics, specifically language acquisition, language change, and language variation, showing how statistical models reveal essential data for theory building and testing. Although these areas have typically used statistical modeling, Abney goes further by addressing the central figure of generative grammar: the adult monolingual speaker. He argues that statistical methods are of great interest even to the theoretical linguist, because the issues they bear on are in fact linguistic *issues, basic to an understanding of human language. Finally, Abney defends the provocative position that a weighted grammar is the correct model for explanation of several central questions in linguistics, such as the nature of parameter setting and degrees of grammaticality.—Eds.*

In the space of the last 10 years, statistical methods have gone from being virtually unknown in computational linguistics to being a fundamental given. In
1996, no one can profess to be a computational linguist without a passing
knowledge of statistical methods. HMM's are as de rigeur as LR tables, and
anyone who cannot at least use the terminology persuasively risks being mistaken for kitchen help at the ACL banquet.

More seriously, statistical techniques have brought significant advances in
broad-coverage language processing. Statistical methods have made real
progress possible on a number of issues that had previously stymied attempts
to liberate systems from toy domains: issues that include disambiguation, error
correction, and the induction of the sheer volume of information requisite for
handling unrestricted text. And the sense of progress has generated a great deal
of enthusiasm for statistical methods in computational linguistics.

However, this enthusiasm has not been catching in linguistics proper. It is
always dangerous to generalize about linguists, but I think it is fair to say that
most linguists are either unaware (and unconcerned) about trends in computational linguistics, or hostile to current developments. The gulf in basic assumptions is simply too wide, with the result that research on the other side can only
seem naive, ill-conceived, and a complete waste of time and money.

In part the difference is a difference of goals. A large part of computational
linguistics focuses on practical applications, and is little concerned with human
language processing. Nonetheless, at least some computational linguists aim to
advance our scientific understanding of the human language faculty by better
understanding the computational properties of language. One of the most interesting and challenging questions about human language computation is just how
people are able to deal so effortlessly with the very issues that make processing
unrestricted text so difficult. Statistical methods provide the most promising
current answers, and as a result the excitement about statistical methods is also
shared by those in the cognitive reaches of computational linguistics.

In this chapter, I would like to communicate some of that excitement to fellow
linguists, or at least, perhaps, to make it comprehensible. There is no denying
that there is a culture clash between theoretical and computational linguistics
that serves to reinforce mutual prejudices. In caricature, computational linguists
believe that by throwing more cycles and more raw text into their statistical
black box, they can dispense with linguists altogether, along with their fanciful
Rube Goldberg theories about exotic linguistic phenomena. The linguist objects
that, even if those black boxes make you oodles of money on speech recognizers and machine-translation programs (which they do not), they fail to advance
our understanding. I will try to explain how statistical methods just might contribute to understanding of the sort that linguists are after.

This paper, then, is essentially an apology, in the old sense of *apology*. I wish to explain why we would do such a thing as to use statistical methods, and why they are not really such a bad thing, maybe not even for linguistics proper.

1 Language Acquisition, Language Variation, and Language Change

I think the most compelling, though least well-developed, arguments for statistical methods in linguistics come from the areas of language acquisition, language variation, and language change.

Language Acquisition   Under standard assumptions about the grammar, we would expect the course of language development to be characterized by abrupt changes, each time the child learns or alters a rule or parameter of the grammar. If, as seems to be the case, changes in child grammar are actually reflected in changes in relative frequencies of structures that extend over months or more, it is hard to avoid the conclusion that the child has a probabilistic or weighted grammar in some form. The form that would perhaps be least offensive to mainstream sensibilities is a grammar in which the child "tries out" rules for a time. During the trial period, both the new and old versions of a rule coexist, and the probability of using one or the other changes with time, until the probability of using the old rule finally drops to zero. At any given point, in this picture, a child's grammar is a stochastic (i.e., probabilistic) grammar.

An aspect of this little illustration that bears emphasizing is that the probabilities are added to a grammar of the usual sort. A large part of what is meant by "statistical methods" in computational linguistics is the study of stochastic grammars of this form: grammars obtained by adding probabilities in a fairly transparent way to "algebraic" (i.e., nonprobabilistic) grammars. Stochastic grammars of this sort do not constitute a rejection of the underlying algebraic grammars, but a supplementation. This is quite different from some uses to which statistical models (most prominently, neural networks) are put, in which attempts are made to model some approximation of linguistic behavior with an undifferentiated network, with the result that it is difficult or impossible to relate the network's behavior to a linguistic understanding of the sort embodied in an algebraic grammar. (It should, however, be pointed out that the problem with such applications does not lie with neural nets, but with the unenlightening way they are sometimes put to use.)

Language Change   Similar comments apply, on a larger scale, to language change. If the units of change are as algebraic grammars lead us to expect—rules or parameters or the like—we would expect abrupt changes. We might expect someone to go down to the local pub one evening, order "Ale!," and be served an eel instead, because the Great Vowel Shift happened to him a day too early.[1] In fact, linguistic changes that are attributed to rule changes or changes of parameter settings take place gradually, over considerable stretches of time measured in decades or centuries. It is more realistic to assume that the language of a speech community is a stochastic composite of the languages of the individual speakers, described by a stochastic grammar. In the stochastic "community" grammar, the probability of a given construction reflects the relative proportion of speakers who use the construction in question. Language change consists in shifts in relative frequency of constructions (rules, parameter settings, etc.) in the community. If we think of speech communities as populations of grammars that vary within certain bounds, and if we think of language change as involving gradual shifts in the center of balance of the grammar population, then statistical models are of immediate applicability [Tabor, 1994].

In this picture, we might still continue to assume that an adult monolingual speaker possesses a particular algebraic grammar, and that stochastic grammars are only relevant for the description of communities of varying grammars. However, we must at least make allowance for the fact that individuals routinely comprehend the language of their community, with all its variance. This rather suggests that at least the grammar used in language comprehension is stochastic. I return to this issue below.

Language Variation   There are two senses of language variation I have in mind here: dialectology, on the one hand, and typology, on the other. It has been suggested that some languages consist of a collection of dialects that blend smoothly one into the other, to the point that the dialects are more or less arbitrary points in a continuum. For example, Tait describes Inuit as "a fairly unbroken chain of dialects, with mutual intelligibility limited to proximity of contact, the furthest extremes of the continuum being unintelligible to each other" [Tait, 1994, p. 3]. To describe the distribution of Latin-American native languages, Kaufman defines a *language complex* as "a geographically continuous zone that contains linguistic diversity greater than that found within a single language . . . , but where internal linguistic boundaries similar to those that separate clearly discrete languages are lacking" [Kaufman, 1994, p. 31]. The continuousness of changes with geographic distance is consistent with the picture of a speech community with grammatical variance, as sketched above. With geographic distance,

---

1. I have read this anecdote somewhere before, but have been unable to find the citation. My apologies to the unknown author.

the mix of frequency of usage of various constructions changes, and a stochastic grammar of some sort is an appropriate model [Kessler, 1995].

Similar comments apply in the area of typology, with a twist. Many of the universals of language that have been identified are statistical rather than absolute, including rough statements about the probability distribution of language features ("head-initial and head-final languages are about equally frequent") or conditional probability distributions ("postpositions in verb-initial languages are more common than prepositions in verb-final languages") [Hawkins, 1983, 1990]. There is as yet no model of how this probability distribution comes about, that is, how it arises from the statistical properties of language change. Which aspects of the distribution are stable, and which would be different if we took a sample of the world's languages 10,000 years ago or 10,000 years hence? There is now a vast body of mathematical work on stochastic processes and the dynamics of complex systems (which includes, but is not exhausted by, work on neural nets), much of which is of immediate relevance to these questions.

In short, it is plausible to think of all of these issues—language acquisition, language change, and language variation—in terms of populations of grammars, whether those populations consist of grammars of different speakers or sets of hypotheses a language learner entertains. When we examine populations of grammars varying within bounds, it is natural to expect statistical models to provide useful tools.

2   Adult Monolingual Speakers

But what about an adult monolingual speaker? Ever since Chomsky, linguistics has been firmly committed to the idealization to an adult monolingual speaker in a homogeneous speech community. Do statistical models have anything to say about language under that idealization?

In a narrow sense, I think the answer is probably not. Statistical methods bear mostly on all the issues that are outside the scope of interest of current mainstream linguistics. In a broader sense, though, I think that says more about the narrowness of the current scope of interest than about the linguistic importance of statistical methods. Statistical methods are of great linguistic interest because the issues they bear on are linguistic issues, and essential to an understanding of what human language is and what makes it tick. We must not forget that the idealizations that Chomsky made were an expedient, a way of managing the vastness of our ignorance. One aspect of language is its algebraic properties, but that is only one aspect of language, and certainly not the only important aspect. Also important are the statistical properties of language communities. And stochastic models are also essential for understanding language production and comprehension, particularly in the presence of variation and noise. (I focus here on comprehension, though considerations of language production have also provided an important impetus for statistical methods in computational linguistics [Smadja, 1989, 1991].)

To a significant degree, I think linguistics has lost sight of its original goal, and turned Chomsky's expedient into an end in itself. Current theoretical syntax gives a systematic account of a very narrow class of data, judgments about the well-formedness of sentences for which the intended structure is specified, where the judgments are adjusted to eliminate gradations of goodness and other complications. Linguistic data other than structure judgments are classified as "performance" data, and the adjustments that are performed on structure-judgment data are deemed to be corrections for "performance effects." Performance is considered the domain of psychologists, or at least, not of concern to linguists.

The term *performance* suggests that the things that the standard theory abstracts away from or ignores are a natural class; they are data that bear on language processing but not language structure. But in fact a good deal that is labeled "performance" is not computational in any essential way. It is more accurate to consider performance to be negatively defined: it is whatever the grammar does not account for. It includes genuinely computational issues, but a good deal more that is not. One issue I would like to discuss in some detail is the issue of grammaticality and ambiguity judgments about sentences as opposed to structures. These judgments are no more or less computational than judgments about structures, but it is difficult to give a good account of them with grammars of the usual sort; they seem to call for stochastic, or at least weighted, grammars.

2.1 Grammaticality and Ambiguity

Consider the following:

(1) a. The a are of I
    b. The cows are grazing in the meadow
    c. John saw Mary

The question is the status of these examples with respect to grammaticality and ambiguity. The judgments here, I think, are crystal clear: (1a) is word salad, and (1b) and (c) are unambiguous sentences.

In point of fact, (1a) is a grammatical noun phrase, and (1b) and (c) are ambiguous, the nonobvious reading being as a noun phrase. Consider: an *are* is a measure of area, as in *a hectare is a hundred ares,* and letters of the alphabet may be used as nouns in English ("*Written on the sheet was a single lowercase a,*" "*As described in section 2, paragraph b . . .*"). Thus (1a) has a structure in which *are* and *I* are head nouns, and *a* is a modifier of *are*. This analysis even becomes perfectly natural in the following scenario. Imagine we are surveyors, and that we have mapped out a piece of land into large segments, designated with capital letters, and subdivided into one-are subsegments, designated with lowercase letters. Then *The a are of I* is a perfectly natural description for a particular parcel on our map.

As for (1b), *are* is again the head noun, *cows* is a premodifier, and *grazing in the meadow* is a postmodifier. It might be objected that plural nouns cannot be nominal premodifiers, but in fact they often are: consider *the bonds market, a securities exchange, he is vice president and media director, an in-home health care services provider, Hartford's claims division, the financial-services industry, its line of systems management software.* (Several of these examples are extracted from the *Wall Street Journal.*)

It may seem that examples (1a) and (b) are illustrative only of a trivial and artificial problem that arises because of a rare usage of a common word. But the problem is not trivial: without an account of "rare usage," we have no way of distinguishing between genuine ambiguities and these spurious ambiguities. Alternatively, one might object that if one does not know that *are* has a reading as a noun, then *are* is actually unambiguous in one's idiolect, and (1a) is genuinely ungrammatical. But in that case the question becomes why *a hectare is a hundred ares* is not judged equally ungrammatical by speakers of the idiolect in question.

Further, (1c) illustrates that the rare usage is not an essential feature of examples (a) and (b). *Saw* has a reading as a noun, which may be less frequent than the verb reading, but is hardly a rare usage. Proper nouns can modify (*Gatling gun*) and be modified by (*Typhoid Mary*) common nouns. Hence, *John saw Mary* has a reading as a noun phrase, referring to the Mary who is associated with a kind of saw called a John saw.

It may be objected that constructions like *Gatling gun* and *Typhoid Mary* belong to the lexicon, not the grammar, but however that may be, they are completely productive. I may not know what *Cohen equations, the Russia house,* or *Abney sentences* are, but if not, then the denotata of *Cohen's equations, the Russian house,* or *those sentences of Abney's* are surely equally unfamiliar.[2]

---

2. There are also syntactic grounds for doubt about the assumption that noun-noun modification belongs to the lexicon. Namely, adjectives can intervene between the modifying noun and the head noun. (Examples are given later in this section.) If adjective modification belongs to the syntax, and if there are no discontinuous words or movement of pieces of lexical items, then at least some modification of nouns by nouns must take place in the syntax.

Likewise I may not know who *pegleg Pete* refers to, or *riverboat Sally,* but that does not make the constructions any less grammatical or productive.

The problem is epidemic, and it snowballs as sentences grow longer. One often hears in computational linguistics about completely unremarkable sentences with hundreds of parses, and that is in fact no exaggeration. Nor is it merely a consequence of having a poor grammar. If one examines the undesired analyses, one generally finds that they are extremely implausible, and often do considerable violence to "soft" constraints like heaviness constraints or the number and sequence of modifiers, but no one piece of the structure is outright ungrammatical.

To illustrate, consider this sentence, drawn more or less at random from a book (Quine's *Word and Object*) drawn more or less at random from my shelf:

(2) In a general way such speculation is epistemologically relevant, as suggesting how organisms maturing and evolving in the physical environment we know might conceivably end up discoursing of abstract objects as we do [Quine, 1960, p. 123].

One of the many spurious structures this sentence might receive is the following:

(3)

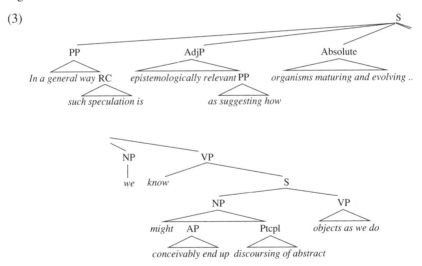

There are any number of criticisms one can direct at this structure, but I believe none of them are fatal. It might be objected that the PP-AdjP-Absolute sequence of sentential premodifiers is illegitimate, but each is individually fine, and there is no hard limit on stacking them. One can even come up with relatively good examples with all three modifiers, e.g. [PP *on the beach*] [AdjP *naked*

as jaybirds] [$_{\text{Absolute}}$ *waves lapping against the shore*] *the wild boys carried out their bizarre rituals.*

Another point of potential criticism is the question of licensing the elided sentence after *how*. In fact its content could either be provided from preceding context or from the rest of the sentence, as in *though as yet unable to explain how, astronomers now know that stars develop from specks of grit in giant oysters.*

Might is taken here as a noun, as in *might and right.* The AP *conceivably end up* may be a bit mysterious: *end up* is here an adjectival, as in *we turned the box end up. Abstract* is unusual as a mass noun, but can in fact be used as one, as, for example, in *the article consisted of three pages of abstract and only two pages of actual text.*

One might object that the NP headed by *might* is bad because of the multiple postmodifiers, but in fact there is no absolute constraint against stacking nominal postmodifiers, and good examples can be constructed with the same structure: *marlinespikes, business end up, sprinkled with tabasco sauce, can be a powerful deterrent against pigeons.* Even the commas are not absolutely required. The strength of preference for them depends on how heavy the modifiers are: cf. *strength judiciously applied increases the effectiveness of diplomacy, a cup of peanuts unshelled in the stock adds character.*[3]

In short, the structure (3) seems to be best characterized as grammatical, though it violates any number of parsing preferences and is completely absurd.

One might think that one could eliminate ambiguities by turning some of the dispreferences into absolute constraints. But attempting to eliminate unwanted readings that way is like squeezing a balloon: every dispreference that is turned into an absolute constraint to eliminate undesired structures has the unfortunate side effect of eliminating the desired structure for some other sentence. No matter how difficult it is to think up a plausible example that violates the constraint, some writer has probably already thought one up by accident, and we will improperly reject his sentence as ungrammatical if we turn the dispreference into an absolute constraint. To illustrate: if a noun is premodified by both an adjective and another noun, standard grammars require the adjective to come first, inasmuch as the noun adjoins to N^0 but the adjective adjoins to $\overline{N}$. It is not easy to think up good examples that violate this constraint. Perhaps the reader would care to try before reading the examples in the footnote.[4]

---

3. Cf. this passage from Tolkien: "Their clothes were mended as well as their bruises their tempers and their hopes. Their bags were filled with food and provisions light to carry but strong to bring them over the mountain passes." [Tolkien, 1966, p. 61]

4. *Maunder climatic cycles, ice-core climatalogical records, a Kleene-star transitive closure, Precambrian era solar activity, highland igneous formations.*

Not only is my absurd analysis (3) arguably grammatical, there are many, many equally absurd analyses to be found. For example, *general* could be a noun (the army officer) instead of an adjective, or *evolving in* could be analyzed as a particle verb, or *the physical* could be a noun phrase (a physical exam)—not to mention various attachment ambiguities for coordination and modifiers, giving a multiplicative effect. The consequence is considerable ambiguity for a sentence that is perceived to be completely unambiguous.

Now perhaps it seems I am being perverse, and I suppose I am. But it is a perversity that is implicit in grammatical descriptions of the usual sort, and it emerges unavoidably as soon as we systematically examine the structures that the grammar assigns to sentences. Either the grammar assigns too many structures to sentences like (2), or it incorrectly predicts that examples like *three pages of abstract* or *a cup of peanuts unshelled in the stock* have no well-formed structure.

To sum up, there is a problem with grammars of the usual sort: their predictions about grammaticality and ambiguity are simply not in accord with human perceptions. The problem of how to identify the correct structure from among the in-principle possible structures provides one of the central motivations for the use of weighted grammars in computational linguistics. A weight is assigned to each aspect of structure permitted by the grammar, and the weight of a particular analysis is the combined weight of the structural features that make it up. The analysis with the greatest weight is predicted to be the perceived analysis for a given sentence.

Before describing in more detail how weighted grammars contribute to a solution to the problem, though, let me address an even more urgent issue: is this even a linguistic problem?

2.2 Is This Linguistics?

Under the usual assumptions, the fact that the grammar predicts grammaticality and ambiguity where none is perceived is not a linguistic problem. The usual opinion is that perception is a matter of performance, and that grammaticality alone does not predict performance; we must also include non-linguistic factors like plausibility and parsing preferences and maybe even probabilities.

Grammaticality and Acceptability   The implication is that *perceptions* of grammaticality and ambiguity are not linguistic data, but performance data. This stance is a bit odd—are not grammaticality judgments perceptions? And what do we mean by "performance data?" It would be one thing if we were talking about data that clearly have to do with the course of linguistic computation, data like response times and reading times, or regressive eye movement frequencies, or even more outlandish things like positron emission tomographic scans or early receptor potential traces. But human perceptions (judgments, intuitions) about grammaticality and ambiguity are classic linguistic data. What makes the judgments concerning examples (1a–c) performance data? All linguistic data are the result of little informal psycholinguistic experiments that linguists perform on themselves, and the experimental materials are questions of the form "Can you say this?" "Does this mean this?" "Is this ambiguous?" "Are these synonymous?"

Part of the answer is that the judgments about examples (1a–c) are judgments about sentences alone rather than about sentences with specified structures. The usual sort of linguistic judgment is a judgment about the goodness of a particular structure, and example sentences are only significant as bearers of the structure in question. If any choice of words and any choice of context can be found that makes for a good sentence, the structure is deemed to be good. The basic data are judgments about structured sentences in context—that is, sentences plus a specification of the intended structure and intended context— but these basic data are used only grouped in sets of structured contextualized sentences having the same (possibly partial) structure. Such a set is defined to be good just in case any structured contextualized sentence it contains is judged to be good. Hence a great deal of linguists' time is spent in trying to find some choice of words and some context to get a clear positive judgment, to show that a structure of interest is good.

As a result, there is actually no intent that the grammar *predict*—that is, generate—individual structured sentence judgments. For a given structured sentence, the grammar only predicts whether there is some sentence with the same structure that is judged to be good.

For the examples (1), then, we should say that the structure

$[_{NP}$ the $[_N$ a$]$ $[_N$ are$]$ $[_{PP}$ of $[_N$ I$]]]$

is indeed grammatical in the technical sense, since it is acceptable in at least one context, and since every piece of the structure is attested in acceptable sentences.

The grouping of data by structure is not the only way that standard grammars fail to predict acceptability and ambiguity judgments. Judgments are rather smoothly graded, but goodness according to the grammar is all-or-nothing. Discrepancies between grammar and data are ignored if they involve sentences containing center embedding, parsing preference violations, garden-path effects, or in general if their badness can be ascribed to "process-ing complexity."[5]

Grammar and Computation   The difference between structure judgments and string judgments is not that the former are "competence data" in some sense and the latter are "performance data." Rather, the distinction rests on a working assumption about how the data are to be explained, namely, that the data are a result of the interaction of grammatical constraints with computational con-straints. Certain aspects of the data are assumed to be reflections of grammatical constraints, and everything else is ascribed to failures of the processor to trans-late grammatical constraints transparently into behavior, whether because of memory limits or heuristic parsing strategies or whatever obscure mechanisms create gradedness of judgments. We are justified in ignoring those aspects of the data that we ascribe to the idiosyncracies of the processor.

But this distinction does not hold up under scrutiny. Dividing the human lan-guage capacity into grammar and processor is only a manner of speaking, a way of dividing things up for theoretical convenience. It is naive to expect the logical grammar/processor division to correspond to any meaningful physiolog-ical division—say, two physically separate neuronal assemblies, one function-ing as a store of grammar rules and the other as an active device that accesses the grammar-rule store in the course of its operation. And even if we *did* believe in a physiological division between grammar and processor, we have no evidence at all to support that belief; it is not a distinction with any empiri-cal content.

A couple of examples might clarify why I say that the grammar/processor distinction is only for theoretical convenience. Grammars and syntactic struc-tures are used to describe computer languages as well as human languages, but typical compilers do not access grammar-rules or construct parse-trees. At the level of description of the operation of the compiler, grammar-rules and parse-trees exist only "virtually" as abstract descriptions of the course of the compu-

---

5. In addition, there are properties of grammaticality judgments of a different sort that are not being modeled, properties that poorly understood and somewhat worrisome. Disagreements arise not infrequently among judges—it is more often the case than not that I disagree with at least some of the judgments reported in syntax papers, and I think my experience is not unusual. Judgments seem to change with changing theoretical assumptions: a sentence that sounds "not too good" when one expects it to be bad may sound "not too bad" if a change in the grammar changes one's expectations. And judg-ments change with exposure. Some constructions that sound terrible on a first exposure improve considerably with time.

tation being performed. What is separately characterized as, say, grammar vs. parsing strategy at the logical level is completely intermingled at the level of compiler operation.

At the other extreme, the constraints that probably have the strongest computational flavor are the parsing strategies that are considered to underlie garden-path effects. But it is equally possible to characterize parsing preferences in grammatical terms. For example, the low attachment strategy can be characterized by assigning a cost to structures of the form $[_{X^{i+1}} X^i\ Y\ Z]$ proportional to the depth of the subtree Y. The optimal structure is the one with the least cost. Nothing depends on how trees are actually computed: the characterization is only in terms of the shapes of trees.

If we wish to make a distinction between competence and computation, an appropriate distinction is between *what* is computed and *how* it is computed. By this measure, most "performance" issues are not computational issues at all. Characterizing the perceptions of grammaticality and ambiguity described in the previous section does not necessarily involve any assumptions about the computations done during sentence perception. It only involves characterizing the set of structures that are perceived as belonging to a given sentence. That can be done, for example, by defining a weighted grammar that assigns costs to trees, and specifying a constant C such that only structures whose cost is within distance C of the best structure are predicted to be perceived. How the set thus defined is actually computed during perception is left completely open.

We may think of competence vs. performance in terms of knowledge vs. computation, but that is merely a manner of speaking. What is really at issue is an idealization of linguistic data for the sake of simplicity.

The Frictionless Plane, Autonomy and Isolation   Appeal is often made to an analogy between competence and frictionless planes in mechanics. Syntacticians focus on the data that they believe to contain the fewest complicating factors, and "clean up" the data to remove what they believe to be remaining complications that obscure simple, general principles of language.

That is proper and laudable, but it is important not to lose sight of the original problem, and not to mistake complexity for irrelevancy. The test of whether the simple principles we think we have found actually have explanatory power is how well they fare in making sense of the larger picture. There is always the danger that the simple principles we arrive at are artifacts of our data selection and data adjustment. For example, it is sometimes remarked how marvelous it is that a biological system like language should be so discrete and clean, but in fact there is abundant gradedness and variability in the original data; the evidence for the discreteness and cleanness of language seems to be mostly evidence we ourselves have planted.

It has long been emphasized that syntax is autonomous. The doctrine is older than Chomsky; for example, Tesnière [Tesnière, 1959, p. 42][6] writes ". . . la syntaxe n'a à chercher sa propre loi qu'en elle-même. Elle est autonome". To illustrate that structure cannot be equated with meaning, he presents the sentence pair:

le signal vert indique le voie libre
le symbole véritable impose le vitesse lissant

The similarity to Chomsky's later but more famous pair

revolutionary new ideas appear infrequently
colorless green ideas sleep furiously

is striking.

But autonomy is not the same as isolation. Syntax is autonomous in the sense that it cannot be reduced to semantics; well-formedness is not identical to meaningfulness. But syntax in the sense of an algebraic grammar is only one piece in an account of language, and it stands or falls on how well it fits into the larger picture.

The Holy Grail   The larger picture, and the ultimate goal of linguistics, is to describe language in the sense of that which is produced in language production, comprehended in language comprehension, acquired in language acquisition, and, in aggregate, that which varies in language variation and changes in language change.

I have always taken the Holy Grail of generative linguistics to be to characterize a class of models, each of which represents a particular (potential or actual) human language L, and characterizes a speaker of L by defining the class of sentences a speaker of L produces, the structures that a speaker of L perceives for sentences; in short, by predicting the linguistic data that characterize a speaker of L.

A "Turing test" for a generative model would be something like the following. If we use the model to generate sentences at random, the sentences that are produced are judged by humans to be clearly sentences of the language—to "sound natural." And in the other direction, if humans judge a sentence (or non-

---

6. The cited work was completed before Tesnière's death in 1954, though it was not published until 1959.

sentence) to have a particular structure, the model should also assign precisely that structure to the sentence.

Natural languages are such that these tests cannot be passed by an un-weighted grammar. An unweighted grammar distinguishes only between grammatical and ungrammatical structures, and that is not enough. "Sounding natural" is a matter of degree. What we must mean by "randomly generating natural-sounding sentences" is that sentences are weighted by the degree to which they sound natural, and we sample sentences with a probability that accords with their weight. Moreover, the structure that people assign to a sentence is the structure they judge to have been intended by the speaker, and that judgment is also a matter of degree. It is not enough for the grammar to define the set of structures that could possibly belong to the sentence; the grammar should predict which structures humans actually perceive, and what the relative weights are in cases where humans are uncertain about which structure the speaker intended.

The long and little of it is, weighted grammars (and other species of statistical methods) characterize language in such a way as to make sense of language production, comprehension, acquisition, variation, and change. These are linguistic, and not computational issues, a fact that is obscured by labeling everything "performance" that is not accounted for by algebraic grammars. What is really at stake with "competence" is a provisional simplifying assumption, or an expression of interest in certain subproblems of linguistics. There is certainly no indicting an expression of interest, but it is important not to lose sight of the larger picture.

3 How Statistics Helps

Accepting that there are divergences between theory and data—for example, the divergence between predicted and perceived ambiguity—and accepting that this is a linguistic problem, and that it is symptomatic of the incompleteness of standard grammars, how does adding weights or probabilities help make up the difference?

Disambiguation As already mentioned, the problem of identifying the correct parse—the parse that humans perceive—among the possible parses is a central application of stochastic grammars in computational linguistics. The problem of defining which analysis is correct is not a computational problem, however; the computational problem is describing an algorithm to compute the correct parse. There are a variety of approaches to the problem of defining the correct parse. A stochastic context-free grammar provides a simple illustration. Consider the sentence *John walks,* and the grammar

(4) 1. S → NP V   .7
     2. S → NP   .3
     3. NP → N   .8
     4. NP → N N   .2
     5. N → John   .6
     6. N → walks   .4
     7. V → walks   1.0

According to grammar (4), *John walks* has two analyses, one as a sentence and one as a noun phrase. (The rule S → NP represents an utterance consisting of a single noun phrase.) The numbers in the rightmost column represent the weights of rules. The weight of an analysis is the product of the weights of the rules used in its derivation. In the sentential analysis of *John walks,* the derivation consists of rules 1, 3, 5, 7, so the weight is $(.7)(.8)(.6)(1.0) = .336$. In the noun-phrase analysis, the rules 2, 4, 5, 6 are used, so the weight is $(.3)(.2)(.6)(.4) = .0144$. The weight for the sentential analysis is much greater, predicting that it is the one perceived. More refined predictions can be obtained by hypothesizing that an utterance is perceived as ambiguous if the next-best case is not too much worse than the best. If "not too much worse" is interpreted as a ratio of, say, not more than 2:1, we predict that *John walks* is perceived as unambiguous, as the ratio between the weights of the parses is 23:1.[7]

Degrees of Grammaticality   Gradations of acceptability are not accommodated in algebraic grammars: a structure is either grammatical or not. The idea of degrees of grammaticality has been entertained from time to time, and some classes of ungrammatical structures are informally considered to be "worse" than others (most notably, Empty Category Principle (ECP) violations vs. subjacency violations). But such degrees of grammaticality as have been considered have not been accorded a formal place in the theory. Empirically, acceptability judgments vary widely across sentences with a given structure, depending on lexical choices and other factors. Factors that cannot be reduced

---

7. The hypothesis that only the best structure (or possibly, structures) are perceptible is somewhat similar to current approaches to syntax in which *grammaticality* is defined as optimal satisfaction of constraints or maximal economy of derivation. But I will not hazard a guess here about whether that similarity is significant or mere happenstance.

to a binary grammaticality distinction are either poorly modeled or ignored in standard syntactic accounts.

Degrees of grammaticality arise as uncertainty in answering the question "Can you say X?" or perhaps more accurately, "If you said X, would you feel you had made an error?" As such, they reflect degrees of error in speech production. The null hypothesis is that the same measure of goodness is used in both speech production and speech comprehension, though it is actually an open question. At any rate, the measure of goodness that is important for speech comprehension is not degree of grammaticality alone, but a global measure that combines degrees of grammaticality with at least naturalness and structural preference (i.e., "parsing strategies").

We must also distinguish degrees of grammaticality, and indeed, global goodness, from the probability of producing a sentence. Measures of goodness and probability are mathematically similar enhancements to algebraic grammars, but goodness alone does not determine probability. For example, for an infinite language, probability must ultimately decrease with length, though arbitrarily long sentences may be perfectly good.

Perhaps one reason that degrees of grammaticality have not found a place in standard theory is the question of where the numbers come from, if we permit continuous degrees of grammaticality. The answer to where the numbers come from is *parameter estimation*. Parameter estimation is well-understood for a number of models of interest, and can be seen psychologically as part of what goes on during language acquisition.

Naturalness   It is a bit difficult to say precisely what I mean by naturalness. A large component is plausibility, but not plausibility in the sense of world knowledge, but rather plausibility in the sense of selectional preferences, that is, semantic sortal preferences that predicates place on their arguments.

Another important component of naturalness is not semantic, though, but simply "how you say it." This is what has been called collocational knowledge, like the fact that one says *strong tea* and *powerful car,* but not vice versa [Smadja, 1991], or that you say *thick accent* in English, but *starker Akzent* ("strong accent") in German.

Though it is difficult to define just what naturalness is, it is not difficult to recognize it. If one generates text at random from an explicit grammar plus lexicon, the shortcomings of the grammar are immediately obvious in the unnatural—even if not ungrammatical—sentences that are produced. It is also clear that naturalness is not at all the same thing as meaningfulness. For example, I think it is clear that *differential structure* is more natural than *differential child,* even though I could not say what a differential structure might be. Or consider the following examples that were in fact generated at random from a grammar:

(5) a. matter-like, complete, alleged strips
       a stratigraphic, dubious scattering
       a far alternative shallow model
    b. indirect photographic-drill sources
       earlier stratigraphically precise minimums
       Europe's cyclic existence

All these examples are about on a par as concerns meaningfulness, but I think the (b) examples are rather more natural than the (a) examples.

Collocations and selectional restrictions have been two important areas of application of statistical methods in computational linguistics. Questions of interest have been both how to include them in a global measure of goodness, and how to induce them distributionally [Resnik, 1993], both as a tool for investigations, and as a model of human learning.

Structural Preferences Structural preferences, or parsing strategies, have already been mentioned. A "longest-match" preference is one example. The example

(6) The emergency crews hate most is domestic violence

is a garden-path because of a strong preference for the longest initial NP, *The emergency crews,* rather than the correct alternative, *The emergency.* (The correct interpretation is: *The emergency* [*that crews hate most*] *is domestic violence.*) The longest-match preference plays an important role in the disprefer-ence for the structure (3) that we examined earlier.

As already mentioned, these preferences can be seen as structural prefer-ences, rather than parsing preferences. They interact with the other factors we have been examining in a global measure of goodness. For example, in (6), an even longer match, *The emergency crews hate,* is actually possible, but it vio-lates the dispreference for having plural nouns as nominal modifiers.

Error Tolerance A remarkable property of human language comprehension is its error tolerance. Many sentences that an algebraic grammar would simply classify as ungrammatical are actually perceived to have a particular structure. A simple example is *we sleeps,* a sentence whose intended structure is obvious, albeit ungrammatical. In fact, an erroneous structure may actually be preferred to a grammatical analysis; consider

(7) Thanks for all you help.

which I believe is preferentially interpreted as an erroneous version of *Thanks for all your help*. However, there is a perfectly grammatical analysis: *Thanks for all those who you help*.

We can make sense of this phenomenon by supposing that a range of error-correction operations are available, though their application imposes a certain cost. This cost is combined with the other factors we have discussed, to determine a global goodness, and the best analysis is chosen. In (7), the cost of error correction is apparently less than the cost of the alternative in unnaturalness or structural dispreference. Generally, error detection and correction are a major selling point for statistical methods. They were primary motivations for Shannon's noisy channel model [Shannon, 1948], which provides the foundation for many computational linguistic techniques.

Learning on the Fly Not only is the language that one is exposed to full of errors, it is produced by others whose grammars and lexica vary from one's own. Frequently, sentences that one encounters can only be analyzed by adding new constructions or lexical entries. For example, when the average person hears *a hectare is a hundred ares,* they deduce that *are* is a noun, and succeed in parsing the sentence. But there are limits to learning on the fly, just as there are limits to error correction. Learning on the fly does not help one parse *the a are of I*.

Learning on the fly can be treated much like error correction. The simplest approach is to admit a space of learning operations—for example, assigning a new part of speech to a word, adding a new subcategorization frame to a verb, etc.—and assign a cost to applications of the learning operations. In this way it is conceptually straightforward to include learning on the fly in a global optimization.

People are clearly capable of error correction and learning on the fly; they are highly desirable abilities given the noise and variance in the typical linguistic environment. They greatly exacerbate the problem of picking out the intended parse for a sentence, because they explode the candidate space even beyond the already large set of candidates that the grammar provides. To explain how it is nonetheless possible to identify the intended parse, there is no serious alternative to the use of weighted grammars.

Lexical Acquisition A final factor that exacerbates the problem of identifying the correct parse is the sheer richness of natural language grammars and lexica. A goal of earlier linguistic work, and one that is still a central goal of the linguistic work that goes on in computational linguistics, is to develop grammars that assign a reasonable syntactic structure to every sentence of English, or as nearly every sentence as possible. This is not a goal that is currently much in fashion in theoretical linguistics. Especially in Government-Binding theory (GB), the development of large fragments has long since been abandoned in favor of the pursuit of deep principles of grammar.

The scope of the problem of identifying the correct parse cannot be appreciated by examining behavior on small fragments, however deeply analyzed. Large fragments are not just small fragments several times over—there is a qualitative change when one begins studying large fragments. As the range of constructions that the grammar accommodates increases, the number of undesired parses for sentences increases dramatically.

In-breadth studies also give a different perspective on the problem of language acquisition. When one attempts to give a systematic account of phrase structure, it becomes clear just how many little facts there are that do not fall out from grand principles, but just have to be learned. The simple, general principles in these cases are not principles of syntax, but principles of acquisition. Examples are the complex constraints on sequencing of prenominal elements in English, or the syntax of date expressions (*Monday June the 4th, Monday June 4, *Monday June the 4, *June 4 Monday*) or the syntax of proper names (*Greene County Sheriff's Deputy Jim Thurmond*), or the syntax of numeral expressions.

The largest piece of what must be learned is the lexicon. If parameter-setting views of syntax acquisition are correct, then learning the syntax (which in this case does not include the low-level messy bits discussed in the previous paragraph) is actually almost trivial. The really hard job is learning the lexicon.

Acquisition of the lexicon is a primary area of application for distributional and statistical approaches to acquisition. Methods have been developed for the acquisition of parts of speech [Brill, 1993; Schütze, 1993], terminological noun compounds [Bourigault, 1992], collocations [Smadja, 1991], support verbs [Grefenstette, 1995], subcategorization frames [Brent, 1991; Manning, 1993], selectional restrictions [Resnik, 1993], and low-level phrase structure rules [Finch, 1993; Smith and Witten, 1993]. These distributional techniques do not so much compete with parameter setting as a model of acquisition, as much as complement it, by addressing issues that parameter-setting accounts pass over in silence. Distributional techniques are also not adequate alone as models of human acquisition—whatever the outcome of the syntactic vs. semantic bootstrapping debate, children clearly do make use of situations and meaning to learn language—but the effectiveness of distributional techniques indicates at least that they might account for a component of human language learning.

4 Objections

There are a couple of general objections to statistical methods that may be lurking in the backs of readers' minds that I would like to address. First is the sentiment that, however relevant and effective statistical methods may be, they are no more than an engineer's approximation, not part of a proper scientific theory. Second is the nagging doubt: did not Chomsky debunk all this ages ago?

4.1 Are Stochastic Models Only for Engineers?

One might admit that one can account for parsing preferences by a probabilistic model, but insist that a probabilistic model is at best an approximation, suitable for engineering but not for science. On this view, we do not need to talk about degrees of grammaticality, or preferences, or degrees of plausibility. Granted, humans perceive only one of the many legal structures for a given sentence, but the perception is completely deterministic. We need only give a proper account of all the factors affecting the judgment.

Consider the example:

Yesterday three shots were fired at Humberto Calvados, personal assistant to the famous tenor Enrique Felicidad, who was in Paris attending to unspecified personal matters.

Suppose for argument's sake that 60% of readers take the tenor to be in Paris, and 40% take the assistant to be in Paris. Or more to the point, suppose a particular informant, John Smith, chooses the low attachment 60% of the time when encountering sentences with precisely this structure (in the absence of an informative context), and low attachment 40% of the time. One could still insist that no probabilistic decision is being made, but rather that there are lexical and semantic differences that we have inappropriately conflated across sentences with "precisely this structure," and if we take account of these other effects, we end up with a deterministic model after all. A probabilistic model is only a stopgap in absence of an account of the missing factors: semantics, pragmatics, what topics I have been talking to other people about lately, how tired I am, whether I ate breakfast this morning.

By this species of argument, stochastic models are practically always a stopgap approximation. Take stochastic queue theory, for example, by which one can give a probabilistic model of how many trucks will be arriving at given depots in a transportation system. One could argue that if we could just model everything about the state of the trucks and the conditions of the roads, the location of every nail that might cause a flat, and every drunk driver that might cause an accident, then we could in principle predict deterministically how many trucks will be arriving at any depot at any time, and there is no need of stochastic queue theory. Stochastic queue theory is only an approximation in lieu of information that it is impractical to collect.

But this argument is flawed. If we have a complex deterministic system, and if we have access to the initial conditions in complete detail, so that we can compute the state of the system unerringly at every point in time, a simpler stochastic description may still be more insightful. To use a dirty word, some properties of the system are genuinely *emergent,* and a stochastic account is not just an approximation, it provides more insight than identifying every deterministic factor. Or to use a different dirty word, it is a *reductionist* error to reject a successful stochastic account and insist that only a more complex, lower-level, deterministic model advances scientific understanding.

4.2   Chomsky v. Shannon

In one's introductory linguistics course, one learns that Chomsky disabused the field once and for all of the notion that there was anything of interest to statistical models of language. But one usually comes away a little fuzzy on the question of what, precisely, he proved.

The arguments of Chomsky's that I know are from "Three Models for the Description of Language" [Chomsky, 1956] and *Syntactic Structures* [Chomsky, 1957] (essentially the same argument repeated in both places), and from the *Handbook of Mathematical Psychology,* chapter 13 [Miller and Chomsky, 1963]. I think the first argument in *Syntactic Structures* is the best known. It goes like this.

It is fair to assume that neither sentence (1) [colorless green ideas sleep furiously] nor (2) [furiously sleep ideas green colorless], (nor indeed any part of these sentences) has ever occurred in an English discourse . . . Yet (1), though nonsensical, is grammatical, while (2) is not. [Chomsky, 1957, p. 16]

This argument only goes through if we assume that if the frequency of a sentence or "part" is zero in a training sample, its probability is zero. But in fact, there is quite a literature on how to estimate the probabilities of events that do not occur in the sample, and in particular how to distinguish real zeros from zeros that just reflect something that is missing by chance.

Chomsky also gives a more general argument:

If we rank the sequences of a given length in order of statistical approximation to English, we will find both grammatical and ungrammatical sequences scattered throughout the list; there appears to be no particular relation between order of approximation and grammaticalness. [Chomsky, 1957, p. 17]

Because for any n, there are sentences with grammatical dependencies spanning more than n words, so that no nth-order statistical approximation can sort out the grammatical from the ungrammatical examples. In a word, you cannot define grammaticality in terms of probability.

It is clear from context that "statistical approximation to English" is a reference to nth-order Markov models, as discussed by Shannon. Chomsky is saying that there is no way to choose n and ϵ such that

for all sentences s, grammatical(s) $\leftrightarrow P_n(s) > \epsilon$

where $P_n(s)$ is the probability of s according to the "best" nth-order approximation to English.

But Shannon himself was careful to call attention to precisely this point: that for any n, there will be some dependencies affecting the well-formedness of a sentence that an nth-order model does not capture. The point of Shannon's approximations is that, as n increases, the total mass of ungrammatical sentences that are erroneously assigned non-zero probability decreases. That is, we *can* in fact define grammaticality in terms of probability, as follows:

grammatical(s) $\leftrightarrow \lim_{n \to \infty} P_n(s) > 0$

A third variant of the argument appears in the *Handbook*. There Chomsky states that parameter estimation is impractical for an nth-order Markov model where n is large enough "to give a reasonable fit to ordinary usage." He emphasizes that the problem is not just an inconvenience for statisticians, but renders the model untenable as a model of human language acquisition: "we cannot seriously propose that a child learns the values of 10^9 parameters in a childhood lasting only 10^8 seconds."

This argument is also only partially valid. If it takes at least a second to estimate each parameter, and parameters are estimated sequentially, the argument is correct. But if parameters are estimated in parallel, say, by a high-dimensional iterative or gradient-pursuit method, all bets are off. Nonetheless, I think even the most hardcore statistical types are willing to admit that Markov models represent a brute force approach, and are not an adequate basis for psychological models of language processing.

However, the inadequacy of Markov models is not that they are statistical, but that they are statistical versions of finite-state automata. Each of Chomsky's arguments turns on the fact that Markov models are finite-state, not on the fact that they are stochastic. None of his criticisms are applicable to stochastic models generally. More sophisticated stochastic models do exist: stochastic context-free grammars are well understood, and stochastic versions of Tree-Adjoining

Grammar [Resnik, 1992], GB [Fordham and Crocker, 1994], and HPSG [Brew, 1995] have been proposed.

In fact, probabilities make Markov models more adequate than their nonprobabilistic counterparts, not less adequate. Markov models are surprisingly effective, given their finite-state substrate. For example, they are the workhorse of speech recognition technology. Stochastic grammars can also be easier to learn than their nonstochastic counterparts. For example, though Gold [Gold, 1967] showed that the class of context-free grammars is not learnable, Horning [Horning, 1969] showed that the class of stochastic context-free grammars *is* learnable.

In short, Chomsky's arguments do not bear at all on the probabilistic nature of Markov models, only on the fact that they are finite-state. His arguments are not by any stretch of the imagination a sweeping condemnation of statistical methods.

5   Conclusion

In closing, let me repeat the main line of argument as concisely as I can. Statistical methods—by which I mean primarily weighted grammars and distributional induction methods—are clearly relevant to language acquisition, language change, language variation, language generation, and language comprehension. Understanding language in this broad sense is the ultimate goal of linguistics.

The issues to which weighted grammars apply, particularly as concerns perception of grammaticality and ambiguity, one may be tempted to dismiss as performance issues. However, the set of issues labeled "performance" are not essentially computational, as one is often led to believe. Rather, "competence" represents a provisional narrowing and simplification of data in order to understand the algebraic properties of language. "Performance" is a misleading term for "everything else." Algebraic methods are inadequate for understanding many important properties of human language, such as the measure of goodness that permits one to identify the correct parse out of a large candidate set in the face of considerable noise.

Many other properties of language, as well, that are mysterious given unweighted grammars, properties such as the gradualness of rule learning, the gradualness of language change, dialect continua, and statistical universals, make a great deal more sense if we assume weighted or stochastic grammars. There is a huge body of mathematical techniques that computational linguists have begun to tap, yielding tremendous progress on previously intransigent problems. The focus in computational linguistics has admittedly been on technology. But the same techniques promise progress on issues concerning the nature of language that have remained mysterious for so long. The time is ripe to apply them.

Acknowledgments

I thank Tilman Hoehle, Graham Katz, Marc Light, and Wolfgang Sternefeld for their comments on an earlier draft of this chapter. All errors and outrageous opinions are, of course, my own.

References

Didier Bourigault. Surface grammatical analysis for the extraction of terminological noun phrases. In *COLING-92*, Vol. 3, pp. 977–981, 1992.

Michael R. Brent. Automatic acquisition of subcategorization frames from untagged, free-text corpora. In *Proceedings of the 29th Annual Meeting of the Association for Computational Linguistics*, pp. 209–214, 1991.

Chris Brew. Stochastic HPSG. In *Proceedings of EACL-95*, 1995.

Eric Brill. *Transformation-Based Learning*. Ph.D. thesis, University of Pennsylvania, Philadelphia, 1993.

Noam Chomsky. Three models for the description of language. *IRE Transactions on Information Theory*, IT-2(3): 113–124, 1956. New York, Institute of Radio Engineers.

Noam Chomsky. *Syntactic Structures*. The Hague, Mouton, 1957.

Noam Chomsky. The logical basis of linguistic theory. In Horace Lunt, editor, *Proceedings of the Ninth International Congress of Linguists*, pp. 914–978, The Hague, Mouton. 1964.

Steven Paul Finch. *Finding Structure in Language*. PhD thesis, University of Edinburgh, 1993.

Andrew Fordham and Matthew Crocker. Parsing with principles and probabilities. In *The Balancing Act: Combining Symbolic and Statistical Approaches to Language*, 1994.

E. Mark Gold. Language identification in the limit. *Information and Control*, 10(5): 447–474, 1967.

Gregory Grefenstette. Corpus-based method for automatic identification of support verbs for nominalizations. In *EACL-95*, 1995.

John A. Hawkins. *Word Order Universals*. New York, Academic Press, 1983.

John A. Hawkins. A parsing theory of word order universals. *Linguistic Inquiry*, 21(2): 223–262, 1990.

James Jay Horning. *A Study of Grammatical Inference*. Ph.D. thesis, Stanford (Computer Science), 1969.

Terrence Kaufman. The native languages of Latin America: general remarks. In Christopher Moseley and R. E. Asher, editors, *Atlas of the World's Languages*, pp. 31–33, London, Routledge, 1994.

Brett Kessler. Computational dialectology in Irish Gaelic. In *EACL-95*, 1995.

Christopher D. Manning. Automatic acquisition of a large subcategorization dictionary from corpora. In *31st Annual Meeting of the Association for Computational Linguistics*, pp. 235–242, 1993.

George A. Miller and Noam Chomsky. Finitary models of language users. In R. D. Luce, R. Bush, and E. Galanter, editors, *Handbook of Mathematical Psychology*, chapter 13. New York, Wiley, 1963.

Philip Resnik. Probabilistic Tree-Adjoining Grammar as a framework for statistical natural language processing. In *COLING-92*, pp. 418–424, 1992.

Philip Resnik. *Selection and Information*. Ph.D. thesis, University of Pennsylvania, Philadelphia, 1993.

Hinrich Schütze. Part-of-speech induction from scratch. In *Proceedings of the 31st Annual Meeting of the Association for Computational Linguistics*, pp. 251–258, 1993.

Claude E. Shannon. A mathematical theory of communication. *The Bell System Technical Journal*, 27(3–4): 379–423, 623–656, 1948.

Frank Smadja. Microcoding the lexicon for language generation. In Uri Zernik, editor, *Lexical Acquisition: Using On-Line Resources to Build a Lexicon*. Cambridge, Mass.: The MIT Press, 1989.

Frank Smadja. *Extracting Collocations from Text. An Application: Language Generation*. Ph.D. thesis, Columbia University, New York, 1991.

Tony C. Smith and Ian H. Witten. Language inference from function words. Manuscript, University of Calgary and University of Waikato, January 1993.

Whitney Tabor. Syntactic Innovation: A Connectionist Model. PhD thesis, Stanford University, 1994.

Mary Tait. North America. In Christopher Moseley and R. E. Asher, editors, *Atlas of the World's Languages*, pp. 3–30, London, Routledge, 1994.

Luciène Tesnière. Éléments de Syntaxe Structurale. 2nd edition. Paris: Klincksieck, 1959.

J. R. R. Tolkien. *The Hobbit*. Boston, Houghton Mifflin, 1966.

Willard van Orman Quine. *Word and Object*. Cambridge, Mass., The MIT Press, 1960.

Victor Yngve. Language as an error correcting code. Technical Report 33:XV, Quarterly Report of the Research Laboratory of Electronics, The Massachusetts Institute of Technology, April 15, 1954, pp. 73–74.

Chapter 2

Qualitative and Quantitative Models of Speech Translation

Hiyan Alshawi

Alshawi achieves two goals in this chapter. First, he challenges the notion that the identification of a statistical-symbolic distinction in language processing is an instance of the empirical vs. rational debate. Second, Alshawi proposes models for speech translation that retain aspects of qualitative design while moving toward incorporating quantitative aspects for structural dependency, lexical transfer, and linear order.

On the topic of the place of the statistical-symbolic distinction in natural language processing, Alshawi points to the fact that rule-based approaches are becoming increasingly probabilistic. However, at the same time, since language is symbolic by nature, the notion of building a "purely" statistical model may not be meaningful. Alshawi suggests that the basis for the contrast is in fact a distinction between qualitative *systems dealing exclusively with combinatoric constraints, and* quantitative *systems dealing with the computation of numerical functions. Of course, the problem still remains of how and where to introduce quantitative modeling into language processing.*

Alshawi proposes a model to do just this, specifically for the language translation task. The design reflects the conventional qualitative transfer approach; that is, starting with a logic-based grammar and lexicon to produce a set of logical forms that are then filtered, passed to a translation component, and then given to a generation component mapping logical forms to surface syntax, which is then fed to the speech synthesizer. Alshawi then methodically analyzes which of these steps would be improved by the introduction of quantitative modeling. His step-by-step analysis, considering specific ways to improve the basic qualitative model, illustrates the variety of possibilities still to be explored in achieving the optimal balance among types of models.—Eds.

1 Introduction

In recent years there has been a resurgence of interest in statistical approaches to natural language processing. Such approaches are not new, witness the statistical approach to machine translation suggested by Weaver [1955], but the current level of interest is largely due to the success of applying hidden Markov models and N-gram language models in speech recognition. This success was directly measurable in terms of word recognition error rates, prompting language processing researchers to seek corresponding improvements in performance and robustness. A speech translation system, which by necessity combines speech and language technology, is a natural place to consider combining the statistical and conventional approaches, and much of this chapter describes probabilistic models of structural language analysis and translation. My aim is to provide an overall model for translation with the best of both worlds. Various factors lead us to conclude that a lexicalist statistical model with dependency relations is well suited to this goal.

As well as this quantitative approach, we consider a constraint, logic-based approach and try to distinguish characteristics that we wish to preserve from those that are best replaced by statistical models. Although perhaps implicit in many conventional approaches to translation, a characterization in logical terms of what is being done is rarely given, so we attempt to make that explicit here, more or less from first principles.

Before proceeding, I first examine some fashionable distinctions in section 2 in order to clarify the issues involved in comparing these approaches. I argue that the important distinction is not so much a rational-empirical or symbolic-statistical distinction but rather a qualitative-quantitative one. This is followed in section 3 by discussion of the logic-based model, in section 4 by the overall quantitative model, in section 5 by monolingual models, in section 6 by translation models, and, in section 7, some conclusions.

I concentrate throughout on what information about language and translation is coded and how it is expressed as logical constraints in one model or statistical parameters in the other. At Bell Laboratories, we have built a speech translation system with the same underlying motivation as the quantitative model presented here. Although the quantitative model used in that system is different from the one presented here, they can both be viewed as statistical models of dependency grammar. In building the system, we had to address a number of issues that are beyond the scope of this chapter, including parameter estimation and the development of efficient search algorithms.

2   Qualitative and Quantitative Models

One contrast often taken for granted is the identification of a statistical-symbolic distinction in language processing as an instance of the empirical vs. rational debate. I believe this contrast has been exaggerated, though historically it has had some validity in terms of accepted practice. Rule-based approaches have become more empirical in a number of ways: First, a more empirical approach is being adopted to grammar development whereby the rule set is modified according to its performance against corpora of natural text (e.g. [Taylor et al., 1989]). Second, there is a class of techniques for learning rules from text, a recent example being [Brill, 1993]. Conversely, it is possible to imagine building a language model in which all probabilities are estimated according to intuition without reference to any real data, giving a probabilistic model that is not empirical.

Most language processing labeled as statistical involves associating real-number–valued parameters to configurations of symbols. This is not surprising given that natural language, at least in written form, is explicitly symbolic. Presumably, classifying a system as symbolic must refer to a different set of (internal) symbols, but even this does not rule out many statistical systems modeling events involving nonterminal categories and word senses. Given that the notion of a symbol, let alone an "internal symbol," is itself a slippery one, it may be unwise to build our theories of language, or even the way we classify different theories, on this notion.

Instead, it would seem that the real contrast driving the shift toward statistics in language processing is a contrast between *qualitative* systems dealing exclusively with combinatoric constraints, and *quantitative* systems that involve computing numerical functions. This bears directly on the problems of brittleness and complexity that discrete approaches to language processing share with, for example, reasoning systems based on traditional logical inference. It relates to the inadequacy of the dominant theories in linguistics to capture "shades" of meaning or degrees of acceptability which are often recognized by people outside the field as important inherent properties of natural language. The qualitative-quantitative distinction can also be seen as underlying the difference between classification systems based on feature specifications, as used in unification formalisms [Shieber, 1986], and clustering based on a variable degree of granularity (e.g. [Pereira et al., 1993]).

It seems unlikely that these continuously variable aspects of fluent natural language can be captured by a purely combinatoric model. This naturally leads to the question of how best to introduce quantitative modeling into language processing. It is not, of course, necessary for the quantities of a quantitative model to be probabilities. For example, we may wish to define real-valued functions on parse trees that reflect the extent to which the trees conform to, say, minimal attachment and parallelism between conjuncts. Such functions have been used in tandem with statistical functions in experiments on disambiguation (e.g. [Alshawi and Carter, 1994]). Another example is connection strengths in neural network approaches to language processing, though it has been shown that certain networks are effectively computing probabilities [Richard and Lippmann, 1991].

Nevertheless, probability theory does offer a coherent and relatively well-understood framework for selecting between uncertain alternatives, making it a natural choice for quantitative language processing. The case for probability theory is strengthened by a well-developed empirical methodology in the form of statistical parameter estimation. There is also the strong connection between probability theory and the formal theory of information and communication, a connection that has been exploited in speech recognition, for example, using the concept of entropy to provide a motivated way of measuring the complexity of a recognition problem [Jelinek et al., 1992].

Even if probability theory remains, as it currently is, the method of choice in making language processing quantitative, this still leaves the field wide open in terms of carving up language processing into an appropriate set of events for probability theory to work with. For translation, a very direct approach using parameters based on surface positions of words in source and target sentences was adopted in the Candide system [Brown et al., 1990]. However, this does not capture important structural properties of natural language. Nor does it take into account generalizations about translation that are independent of the exact word order in source and target sentences. Such generalizations are, of course, central to qualitative structural approaches to translation (e.g. [Isabelle and Macklovitch, 1986; Alshawi et al., 1992]).

The aim of the quantitative language and translation models presented in sections 5 and 6 is to employ probabilistic parameters that reflect linguistic structure without discarding rich lexical information or making the models too complex to train automatically. In terms of a traditional classification, this would be seen as a "hybrid symbolic-statistical" system because it deals with linguistic structure. From our perspective, it can be seen as a quantitative version of the logic-based model because both models attempt to capture similar information (about the organization of words into phrases and relations holding between these phrases or their referents), though the tools of modeling are substantially different.

3   Dissecting a Logic-Based System

We now consider a hypothetical speech translation system in which the language processing components follow a conventional qualitative transfer design. Although hypothetical, this design and its components are similar to those used in existing database query [Rayner and Alshawi, 1992] and translation systems [Alshawi et al., 1992]. More recent versions of these systems have been gradually taking on a more quantitative flavor, particularly with respect to choosing between alternative analyses, but our hypothetical system will be more purist in its qualitative approach.

The overall design is as follows. We assume that a speech recognition subsystem delivers a list of text strings corresponding to transcriptions of an input utterance. These recognition hypotheses are passed to a parser which applies a logic-based grammar and lexicon to produce a set of logical forms, specifically formulas in first order logic corresponding to possible interpretations of the utterance. The logical forms are filtered by contextual and word-sense constraints, and one of them is passed to the translation component. The translation relation is expressed by a set of first order axioms which are used by a theorem prover to derive a target language logical form that is equivalent (in some context) to the source logical form. A grammar for the target language is then applied to the target form, generating a syntax tree whose fringe is passed to a speech synthesizer.

Taking the various components in turn, we make a note of undesirable properties that might be improved by quantitative modeling.

3.1   Analysis and Generation

A grammar, expressed as a set of syntactic rules (axioms) G_{syn} and a set of semantic rules (axioms) G_{sem} is used to support a relation *form* holding between strings s and logical forms ϕ expressed in first order logic:

$$G_{syn} \cup G_{sem} \models form(s, \phi)$$

The relation *form* is many-to-many, associating a string with linguistically possible logical form interpretations. In the analysis direction, we are given s and search for logical forms ϕ, while in generation we search for strings s given ϕ.

For analysis and generation, we are treating strings s and logical forms ϕ as object level entities. In interpretation and translation, we will move down from this meta-level reasoning to reasoning with the logical forms as propositions.

The list of text strings handed by the recognizer to the parser can be assumed to be ordered in accordance with some acoustic scoring scheme internal to the recognizer. The magnitude of the scores is ignored by our qualitative language processor; it simply processes the hypotheses one at a time until it finds one for which it can produce a complete logical form interpretation that passes grammatical and interpretation constraints, at which point it discards the remaining hypotheses. Clearly, discarding the acoustic score and taking the first hypothesis that satisfies the constraints may lead to an interpretation that is less plausible than one derivable from a hypothesis further down in the recognition list. But there is no point in processing these later hypotheses since we will be forced to select one interpretation essentially at random.

Syntax   The syntactic rules in G_{syn} relate "category" predicates c_0, c_1, c_2 holding of a string and two spanning substrings (we limit the rules here to two daughters for simplicity):

$$c_0(s_0) \wedge daughters(s_0, s_1, s_2) \leftarrow$$
$$c_1(s_1) \wedge c_2(s_2) \wedge (s_0 = concat(s_1, s_2))$$

(Here, and subsequently, variables like s_0 and s_1 are implicitly universally quantified.) G_{syn} also includes lexical axioms for particular strings w consisting of single words:

$$c_1(w), \quad \ldots \quad c_m(w)$$

For a feature-based grammar, these rules can include conjuncts constraining the values, $a_1, a_2, \ldots$, of discrete-valued functions f on the strings:

$$f(w) = a_1, \quad f(s_0) = f(s_1)$$

The main problem here is that such grammars have no notion of a degree of grammatical acceptability—a sentence is either grammatical or ungrammatical. For small grammars this means that perfectly acceptable strings are often rejected; for large grammars we get a vast number of alternative trees so the chance of selecting the correct tree for simple sentences can get worse as the grammar coverage increases. There is also the problem of requiring increasingly complex feature sets to describe idiosyncrasies in the lexicon.

Semantics   Semantic grammar axioms belonging to G_{sem} specify a "composition" function g for deriving a logical form for a phrase from those for its subphrases:

$$form(s_0, g(\phi_1, \phi_2)) \leftarrow$$
$$daughters(s_0, s_1, s_2) \wedge c_1(s_1) \wedge c_2(s_2) \wedge c_0(s_0)$$
$$\wedge form(s_1, \phi_1) \wedge form(s_2, \phi_2)$$

The interpretation rules for strings bottom out in a set of lexical semantic rules associating words with predicates ($p_1, p_2, \ldots$) corresponding to "word senses." For a particular word and syntactic category, there will be a (small, possibly empty) finite set of such word-sense predicates:

$$c_i(w) \rightarrow form\left(w, p_1^i\right)$$

$$\ldots$$

$$c_i(w) \rightarrow form\left(w, p_m^i\right)$$

First order logic was assumed as the semantic representation language because it comes with well-understood, if not very practical, inferential machinery for constraint solving. However, applying this machinery requires making logical forms fine-grained to a degree often not warranted by the information the speaker of an utterance intended to convey. An example of this is explicit scoping which leads (again) to large numbers of alternatives which the qualitative model has difficulty choosing between. Also, many natural language sentences cannot be expressed in first order logic without resort to elaborate formulas requiring complex semantic composition rules. These rules can be simplified by using a higher order logic but at the expense of even less practical inferential machinery.

In applying the grammar in generation we are faced with the problem of balancing over- and undergeneration by tweaking grammatical constraints, there being no way to prefer fully grammatical target sentences over more marginal ones. Qualitative approaches to grammar tend to emphasize the ability to capture generalizations as the main measure of success in linguistic modeling. This might explain why producing appropriate lexical collocations is rarely addressed seriously in these models, even though lexical collocations are important for fluent generation. The study of collocations for generation fits in more naturally with statistical techniques, as illustrated by Smajda and McKeown [1990].

3.2   Interpretation

In the logic-based model, interpretation is the process of identifying from the possible interpretations ϕ of s for which $form(s, \phi)$ hold, ones that are consistent with the context of interpretation. We can state this as follows:

$$R \cup S \cup A \models \phi$$

Here, we have separated the context into a contingent set of contextual propositions S and a set R of (monolingual) "meaning postulates," or selectional restrictions, that constrain the word sense predicates in all contexts. A is a set of assumptions sufficient to support the interpretation ϕ given S and R. In other words, this is "interpretation as abduction" [Hobbs et al., 1988], since abduction, not deduction, is needed to arrive at the assumptions A.

The most common types of meaning postulates in R are those for restriction, hyponymy, and disjointness, expressed as follows:

$p_1(x_1, x_2) \rightarrow p_2(x_1)$ restriction
$p_2(x) \rightarrow p_3(x)$ hyponymy
$\neg(p_3(x) \wedge p_4(x))$ disjointness

Although there are compilation techniques (e.g. [Mellish, 1988]) which allow selectional constraints stated in this fashion to be implemented efficiently, the scheme is problematic in other respects. To start with, the assumption of a small set of senses for a word is at best awkward because it is difficult to arrive at an optimal granularity for sense distinctions. Disambiguation with selectional restrictions expressed as meaning postulates is also problematic because it is virtually impossible to devise a set of postulates that will always filter all but one alternative. We are thus forced to underfilter and make an arbitrary choice between remaining alternatives.

3.3 Logic-Based Translation

In both the quantitative and qualitative models we take a transfer approach to translation. We do not depend on interlingual symbols, but instead map a representation with constants associated with the source language into a corresponding expression with constants from the target language. For the qualitative model, the operable notion of correspondence is based on logical equivalence and the constants are source word-sense predicates $p_1, p_2, \ldots$ and target sense predicates $q_1, q_2, \ldots$.

More specifically, we will say the translation relation between a source logical form ϕ_s and a target logical form ϕ_t holds if we have

$$B \cup S \cup A' \models (\phi_s \leftrightarrow \phi_t)$$

where B is a set of monolingual and bilingual meaning postulates, and S is a set of formulas characterizing the current context. A' is a set of assumptions that includes the assumptions A which supported ϕ_s. Here bilingual meaning postulates are first order axioms relating source and target-sense predicates. A typical bilingual postulate for translating between p_1 and q_1 might be of the form:

$$p_5(x_1) \rightarrow (p_1(x_1, x_2) \leftrightarrow q_1(x_1, x_2))$$

The need for the assumptions A' arises when a source language word is vaguer than its possible translations in the target language, so different choices of target words will correspond to translations under different assumptions. For example, the condition $p_5(x_1)$ above might be proved from the input logical form, or it might need to be assumed.

In the general case, finding solutions (i.e. A', ϕ_t pairs) for the abductive schema is an undecidable theorem-proving problem. This can be alleviated by placing restrictions on the form of meaning postulates and input formulas and using heuristic search methods. Although such an approach was applied with some success in a limited-domain system translating logical forms into database queries [Rayner and Alshawi, 1992], it is likely to be impractical for language translation with tens of thousands of sense predicates and related axioms.

Setting aside the intractability issue, this approach does not offer a principled way of choosing between alternative solutions proposed by the prover. One would like to prefer solutions with "minimal" sets of assumptions, but it is difficult to find motivated definitions for this minimization in a purely qualitative framework.

4 Quantitative Model Components

4.1 Moving to a Quantitative Model
In moving to a quantitative architecture, we propose to retain many of the basic characteristics of the qualitative model:

- A transfer organization with analysis, transfer, and generation components
- Monolingual models that can be used for both analysis and generation
- Translation models that exclusively code contrastive (cross-linguistic) information
- Hierarchical phrases capturing recursive linguistic structure

Instead of feature-based syntax trees and first order logical forms we will adopt a simpler, monostratal representation that is more closely related to those found in dependency grammars (e.g. [Hudson, 1984]). Dependency representations have been used in large-scale qualitative machine translation systems, notably by McCord [1988]. The notion of a lexical "head" of a phrase is central to these representations because they concentrate on relations between such lexical heads. In our case, the dependency representation is monostratal in that the relations may include ones normally classified as belonging to syntax, semantics, or pragmatics.

One salient property of our language model is that it is strongly lexical: it consists of statistical parameters associated with relations between lexical items and the number and ordering of dependents of lexical heads. This lexical anchoring facilitates statistical training and sensitivity to lexical variation and collocations. In order to gain the benefits of probabilistic modeling, we replace the task of developing large rule sets with the task of estimating large numbers of statistical parameters for the monolingual and translation models. This gives rise to a new cost tradeoff in human annotation and judgment vs. barely tractable fully automatic training. It also necessitates further research on lexical similarity and clustering (e.g. [Pereira et al., 1993; Dagan et al., 1993]) to improve parameter estimation from sparse data.

We should emphasize at the outset that the quantitative model presented below is not a way of augmenting a logic-based system by associating probabilities or costs with the axioms or rules of that model. Instead, the parameters of the quantitative model encode all the structural and preference information necessary to apply the model.

4.2   Translation via Lexical Relation Graphs

The model associates phrases with *relation graphs*. A relation graph is a directed labeled graph consisting of a set of *relation edges*. Each edge has the form of an atomic proposition

$r(w_i, w_j)$

where r is a relation symbol, w_i is the lexical head of a phrase, and w_j is the lexical head of another phrase (typically a subphrase of the phrase headed by w_i). The nodes w_i and w_j are word occurrences representable by a word and an index, the indices uniquely identifying particular occurrences of the words in a discourse or corpus. The set of relation symbols is open-ended, but the first argument of the relation is always interpreted as the *head* and the second as the *dependent* with respect to this relation. The relations in the models for the source and target languages need not be the same, or even overlap. To keep the language models simple, we will mainly restrict ourselves here to dependency graphs that are trees with unordered siblings. In particular, phrases will always be contiguous strings of words and dependents will always be heads of subphrases.

Ignoring algorithmic issues relating to compactly representing and efficiently searching the space of alternative hypotheses, the overall design of the quantitative system is as follows. The speech recognizer produces a set of word-position hypotheses (perhaps in the form of a word lattice) corresponding to a set of string hypotheses for the input. The source language model is used to compute a set of possible relation graphs, with associated probabilities, for each string hypothesis. A probabilistic graph translation model then provides, for each source relation graph, the probabilities of deriving corresponding graphs with word occurrences from the target language. These target graphs include all the words of possible translations of the utterance hypotheses but do not specify the surface order of these words. Probabilities for different possible word orderings are computed according to ordering parameters which form part of the target language model.

In the following subsection we explain how the probabilities for these various processing stages are combined to select the most likely target word sequence. This word sequence can then be handed to the speech synthesizer. For tighter integration between generation and synthesis, information about the derivation of the target utterance can also be passed to the synthesizer.

4.3 Integrated Statistical Model

The probabilities associated with phrases in the above description are computed according to the statistical models for analysis, translation, and generation. In this subsection we show the relationship between these models to arrive at an overall statistical model of speech translation. We are not considering training issues in this paper, though a number of now familiar techniques ranging from methods for unsupervised maximum likelihood estimation to direct estimation using fully annotated data are applicable.

The objects involved in the overall model are as follows (we omit target speech synthesis under the assumption that it proceeds deterministically from a target language word string):

- A_s: (acoustic evidence for) source language speech
- W_s: source language word string
- W_t: target language word string
- C_s: source language relation graph
- C_t: target language relation graph

Given a spoken input in the source language, we wish to find a target language string that is the most likely translation of the input. We are thus interested in the conditional probability of W_t given A_s. This conditional probability can be expressed as follows (cf. [Chang and Su, 1993]):

$$P(W_t \mid A_s) =$$
$$\sum_{W_s, C_s, C_t} P(W_s \mid A_s) \, P(C_s \mid W_s, A_s)$$
$$P(C_t \mid C_s, W_s, A_s) \, P(W_t \mid C_t, C_s, W_s, A_s)$$

We now apply some simplifying independence assumptions concerning relation graphs: specifically, that their derivation from word strings is independent of acoustic information; that their translation is independent of the original words and acoustics involved; and that target word string generation from target relation edges is independent of the source language representations. The extent to which these (Markovian) assumptions hold depends on the extent to which relation edges represent all the relevant information for translation. In particular it means they should express aspects of surface relevant to meaning, such as topicalization, as well as predicate argument structure. In any case, the simplifying assumptions give the following:

$$P(W_t \mid A_s) \simeq$$

$$\sum_{W_s, C_s, C_t} P(W_s \mid A_s) \, P(C_s \mid W_s) \, P(C_t \mid C_s) \, P(W_t \mid C_t)$$

This can be rewritten with two applications of Bayes's rule:

$$\sum_{W_s, C_s, C_t} P(A_s \mid W_s) \, (1/P(A_s)) \, P(W_s \mid C_s)$$

$$P(C_s) \, P(C_t \mid C_s) \, P(W_t \mid C_t)$$

Since A_s is given, $1/P(A_s)$ is a constant which can be ignored in finding the maximum of $P(W_t \mid A_s)$. Determining W_t that maximizes $P(W_t \mid A_s)$ therefore involves the following factors:

- $P(A_s \mid W_s)$: source language acoustics
- $P(W_s \mid C_s)$: source language generation
- $P(C_s)$: source content relations
- $P(C_t \mid C_s)$: source-to-target transfer
- $P(W_t \mid C_t)$: target language generation

We assume that the speech recognizer provides acoustic scores proportional to $P(A_s \mid W_s)$ (or logs thereof). Such scores are normally computed by speech recognition systems, although they are usually also multiplied by word-based language model probabilities $P(W_s)$ which we do not require in this application context. Our approach to language modeling, which covers the content analysis and language generation factors, is presented in section 5 and the transfer probabilities fall under the translation model of section 6.

Finally note that by another application of Bayes's rule we can replace the two factors $P(C_s)P(C_t \mid C_s)$ by $P(C_t)P(C_s \mid C_t)$ without changing other parts of the model. This latter formulation allows us to apply constraints imposed by the target language model to filter inappropriate possibilities suggested by analysis and transfer. In some respects this is similar to Dagan and Itai's approach [1994] to word-sense disambiguation using statistical associations in a second language.

5 Language Models

5.1 Language Production Model

Our language model can be viewed in terms of a probabilistic generative process based on the choice of lexical "heads" of phrases and the recursive generation of subphrases and their ordering. For this purpose, we can define the headword of a phrase to be the word that most strongly influences the way the phrase may be combined with other phrases. This notion has been central to a number of approaches to grammar for some time, including theories like dependency grammar [Hudson, 1984] and HPSG [Pollard and Sag, 1987]. More recently, the statistical properties of associations between words, and more particularly heads of phrases, has become an active area of research (e.g. [Chang et al., 1992; Hindle and Rooth, 1993]).

The language model factors the statistical derivation of a sentence with word string W as follows:

$$P(W) = \sum_C P(C)\, P(W \mid C)$$

where C ranges over relation graphs. The content model, $P(C)$, and generation model, $P(W \mid C)$, are components of the overall statistical model for spoken language translation given earlier. This decomposition of $P(W)$ can be viewed as first deciding on the content of a sentence, formulated as a set of relation edges according to a statistical model for $P(C)$, and then deciding on word order according to $P(W \mid C)$.

Of course, this decomposition simplifies the realities of language production in that real language is always generated in the context of some situation S (real or imaginary), so a more comprehensive model would be concerned with $P(C \mid S)$, that is, language production in context. This is less important, however, in the translation setting since we produce C_t in the context of a source relation graph C_s and we assume the availability of a model for $P(C_t \mid C_s)$.

5.2 Content Derivation Model

The model for deriving the relation graph of a phrase is taken to consist of choosing a lexical head h_0 for the phrase (what the phrase is "about") followed by a series of "node expansion" steps. An expansion step takes a node and chooses a possibly empty set of edges (relation labels and ending nodes) starting from that node. Here we consider only the case of relation graphs that are trees with unordered siblings.

To start with, let us take the simplified case where a head word h has no optional or duplicated dependents (i.e., exactly one for each relation). There will be a set of edges

$$E(h) = \{r_1(h, w_1), r_2(h, w_2)...r_k(h, w_k)\}$$

corresponding to the local tree rooted at h with dependent nodes $w_1...w_k$. The set of relation edges for the entire derivation is the union of these local edge sets.

To determine the probability of deriving a relation graph C for a phrase headed by h_0 we make use of parameters ("dependency parameters")

$$P(r(h, w) \mid h, r)$$

for the probability, given a node h and a relation r, that w is an r-dependent of h. Under the assumption that the dependents of a head are chosen independently from one another, the probability of deriving C is:

$$P(C) = P(Top(h_0)) \prod_{r(h, w) \in C} P(r(h, w) \mid h, r)$$

where $P(Top(h_0))$ is the probability of choosing h_0 to start the derivation.

If we now remove the assumption made earlier that there is exactly one r-dependent of a head, we need to elaborate the derivation model to include choosing the number of such dependents. We model this by parameters

$$P(N(r, n) \mid h)$$

that is, the probability that head h has n r-dependents. We will refer to this probability as a "detail parameter." Our previous assumption amounted to stating that this was always 1 for $n = 1$ or for $n = 0$. Detail parameters allow us to model, for example, the number of adjectival modifiers of a noun or the "degree" to which a particular argument of a verb is optional. The probability of an expansion of h giving rise to local edges $E(h)$ is now:

$$P(E(h) \mid h) =$$

$$\prod_r P(N(r, n_r) \mid h) \; k(n_r) \prod_{1 \leq i \leq n_r} P\big(r(h, w_i^r) \mid h, r\big)$$

where r ranges over the set of relation labels and h has n_r r-dependents $w_1^r...w_n^r$. $k(n_r)$ is a combinatoric constant for taking account of the fact that we are not distinguishing permutations of the dependents (e.g., there are $n_r!$ permutations of the r-dependents of h if these dependents are all distinct).

So if h_0 is the root of a tree C, we have

$$P(C) = P(Top(h_0)) \prod_{h \in heads(C)} P(E_C(h) \mid h)$$

where $heads(C)$ is the set of nodes in C and $E_C(h)$ is the set of edges headed by h in C.

The above formulation is only an approximation for relation graphs that are not trees because the independence assumptions which allow the dependency parameters to be simply multiplied together no longer hold for the general case. Dependency graphs with cycles do arise as the most natural analyses of certain linguistic constructions, but calculating their probabilities on a node-by-node basis as above may still provide probability estimates that are accurate enough for practical purposes.

5.3   Generation Model

We now return to the generation model $P(W \mid C)$. As mentioned earlier, since C includes the words in W and a set of relations between them, the generation model is concerned only with surface order. One possibility is to use "bi-relation" parameters for the probability that an r_i-dependent immediately follows an r_j-dependent. This approach is problematic for our overall statistical model because such parameters are not independent of the "detail" parameters specifying the number of r-dependents of a head.

We therefore adopt the use of "sequencing" parameters, these being probabilities of particular orderings of dependents given that the multiset of dependency relations is known. We let the identity relation e stand for the head itself. Specifically, we have parameters

$$P(s \mid M(s))$$

where s is a sequence of relation labels including an occurrence of e and $M(s)$ is the multiset for this sequence. For a head h in a relation graph C, let s_{WCh} be the sequence of dependent relations induced by a particular word string W generated from C. We now have

$$P(W \mid C) = \prod_{h \in W} \left(\prod_r \frac{1}{k(n_r)} \right) P(s_{WCh} \mid M(s_{WCh}))$$

where h ranges over all the heads in C, and n_r is the number of occurrences of r in s_{WCh}, assuming that all orderings of n_r-dependents are equally likely. We can thus use these sequencing parameters directly in our overall model.

To summarize, our monolingual models are specified by:

- Topmost head parameters $P(Top(h))$
- Dependency parameters $P(r(h, w) \mid h, r)$

- Detail parameters $P(N(r, n) \mid h)$
- Sequencing parameters $P(s \mid M(s))$

The overall model splits the contributions of content $P(C)$ and ordering $P(W \mid C)$. However, we may also want a model for $P(W)$, for example, for pruning speech-recognition hypotheses. Combining our content and ordering models we get:

$$P(W) = \sum_{C} P(C) \, P(W \mid C)$$
$$= \sum_{C} P(Top(h_C)) \prod_{h \in W} P(s_{WCh} \mid h)$$
$$\prod_{r(h, w) \in E_C(h)} P(r(h, w) \mid h, r)$$

The parameters $P(s \mid h)$ can be derived by combining sequencing parameters with the detail parameters for h.

6   Translation Model

6.1   Mapping Relation Graphs

As already mentioned, the translation model defines mappings between relation graphs C_s for the source language and C_t for the target language. A direct (though incomplete) justification of translation via relation graphs may be based on a simple referential view of natural language semantics. Thus nominals and their modifiers pick out entities in a (real or imaginary) world; verbs and their modifiers refer to actions or events in which the entities participate in roles indicated by the edge relations. On this view, the purpose of the translation mapping is to determine a target language relation graph that provides the best approximation to the referential function induced by the source relation graph. We call this approximating referential equivalence.

This referential view of semantics is not adequate for taking account of much of the complexity of natural language, including many aspects of quantification, distributivity, and modality. This means it cannot capture some of the subtleties that a theory based on logical equivalence might be expected to. On the other hand, when we proposed a logic-based approach as our qualitative model, we had to restrict it to a simple first order logic anyway for computational reasons, and even then it did not appear to be practical. Thus using the more impoverished lexical relations representation may not be costing us much in practice.

One aspect of the representation that is particularly useful in the translation application is its convenience for partial or incremental representation of content—we can refine the representation by the addition of further edges. A fully specified denotation of the meaning of a sentence is rarely required for translation, and as we pointed out when discussing logic representations, a complete specification may not have been intended by the speaker. Although we have not provided a denotational semantics for sets of relation edges, we anticipate that this will be possible along the lines developed in monotonic semantics [Alshawi and Crouch, 1992].

6.2 Translation Parameters

To be practical, a model for $P(C_t \mid C_s)$ needs to decompose the source and target graphs C_s and C_t into subgraphs small enough that subgraph translation parameters can be estimated. We do this with the help of "node alignment relations" between the nodes of these graphs. These alignment relations are similar in some respects to the alignments used by Brown et al. [1990] in their surface translation model. The translation probability is then the sum of probabilities over different alignments f:

$$P(C_t \mid C_s) = \sum_f P(C_t, f \mid C_s).$$

There are different ways to model $P(C_t, f \mid C_s)$ corresponding to different kinds of alignment relations and different independence assumptions about the translation mapping.

For our quantitative design, we adopt a simple model in which lexical and relation (structural) probabilities are assumed to be independent. In this model the alignment relations are functions from the word occurrence nodes of C_t to the word occurrences of C_s. The idea is that $f(v_j) = w_i$ means that the source word occurrence w_i "gave rise" to the target word occurrence v_j. The inverse relation f^{-1} need not be a function, allowing different numbers of words in the source and target sentences.

We decompose $P(C_t, f \mid C_s)$ into "lexical" and "structural" probabilities as follows:

$$P(C_t, f \mid C_s) = P(N_t, f \mid N_s)P(E_t \mid N_t, f, C_s)$$

where N_t and N_s are the node sets for C_t and C_s respectively, and E_t is the set of edges for the target graph.

The first factor $P(N_t, f \mid N_s)$ is the lexical component in that it does not take into account any of the relations in the source graph C_s. This lexical component is the product of alignment probabilities for each node of N_s:

$$P(N_t, f \mid N_s) =$$
$$\prod_{w_i \in N_s} P(f^{-1}(w_i) = \{v_i^1 \ldots v_i^n\} \mid w_i).$$

That is, the probability that f maps exactly the (possibly empty) subset $\{v_i^1 \ldots v_i^n\}$ of N_t to w_i. These sets are assumed to be disjoint for different source graph nodes, so we can replace the factors in the above product with parameters:

$$P(M \mid w)$$

where w is a source language word and M is a multiset of target language words.

We will derive a target set of edges E_t of C_t by k derivation steps which partition the set of source edges E_s into subgraphs $S_1 \ldots S_k$. These subgraphs give rise to disjoint sets of relation edges $T_1 \ldots T_k$ which together form E_t. The structural component of our translation model will be the sum of derivation probabilities for such an edge set E_t.

For simplicity, we assume here that the source graph C_s is a tree. This is consistent with our earlier assumptions about the source language model. We take our partitions of the source graph to be the edge sets for local trees. This ensures that the partitioning is deterministic so the probability of a derivation is the product of the probabilities of derivation steps. More complex models with larger partitions rooted at a node are possible, but these require additional parameters for partitioning. For the simple model it remains to specify derivation step probabilities.

The probability of a derivation step is given by parameters of the form:

$$P\big(T_i' \mid S_i', f_i\big)$$

where S_i' and T_i' are unlabeled graphs and f_i is a node alignment function from T_i' to S_i'. Unlabeled graphs are just like our relation edge graphs except that the nodes are not labeled with words (the edges still have relation labels). To apply a derivation step we need a notion of graph matching that respects edge labels: g is an isomorphism (modulo node labels) from a graph G to a graph H if g is a one-one and onto function from the nodes of G to the nodes of H such that

$$r(a, b) \in G \quad \text{iff} \quad r(g(a), g(b)) \in H.$$

The derivation step with parameter $P\big(T_i' \mid S_i', f_i\big)$ is applicable to the source edges S_i, under the alignment f, giving rise to the target edges T_i if (i) there is an isomorphism h_i from S_i' to S_i, (ii) there is an isomorphism g_i from T_i to T_i', and (iii) for any node v of T_i it must be the case that

$$h_i(f_i(g_i(v))) = f(v).$$

This last condition ensures that the target graph partitions join up in a way that is compatible with the node alignment f.

The factoring of the translation model into these lexical and structural components means that it will overgenerate because these aspects are not independent in translation between real natural languages. It is therefore appropriate to filter translation hypotheses by rescoring according to the version of the overall statistical model that included the factors $P(C_t)P(C_s \mid C_t)$ so that the target language model constrains the output of the translation model. Of course, in this case we need to model the translation relation in the "reverse" direction. This can be done in a parallel fashion to the forward direction described above.

7   Conclusions

Our qualitative and quantitative models have a similar overall structure and there are clear parallels between the factoring of logical constraints and statistical parameters, for example, monolingual postulates and dependency parameters, bilingual postulates and translation parameters. The parallelism would have been closer if we had adopted ID/LP style rules [Gazdar et al., 1985] in the qualitative model. However, we argued in section 3 that our qualitative model suffered from lack of robustness, from having only the crudest means for choosing between competing hypotheses, and from being computationally intractable for large vocabularies.

The quantitative model is in a much better position to cope with these problems. It is less brittle because statistical associations have replaced constraints (featural, selectional, etc.) that must be satisfied exactly. The probabilistic models give us a systematic and well-motivated way of ranking alternative hypotheses. Computationally, the quantitative model lets us escape from the undecidability of logic-based reasoning. Because this model is highly lexical, we can hope that the input words will allow effective pruning by limiting the number of search paths having significantly high probabilities.

We retained some of the basic assumptions about the structure of language when moving to the quantitative model. In particular, we preserved the notion of hierarchical phrase structure. Relations motivated by dependency grammar made it possible to do this without giving up sensitivity to lexical collocations which underpin simple statistical models like N-grams. The quantitative model also reduced overall complexity in terms of the sets of symbols used. In addition to words, it only required symbols for dependency relations, whereas the qualitative model required symbol sets for linguistic categories and features, and a set of word sense symbols. Despite their apparent importance to translation, the quantitative system can avoid the use of word-sense symbols (and the problems of granularity they give rise to) by exploiting statistical associations between words in the target language to filter implicit sense choices.

Finally, here is a summary of our reasons for combining statistical methods with dependency representations in our language and translation models:

• Inherent lexical sensitivity of dependency representations, facilitating parameter estimation
• Quantitative preference based on probabilistic derivation and translation
• Incremental or partial, or incremental and partial, specification of the content of utterances, particularly useful in translation
• Decomposition of complex utterances through recursive linguistic structure

These factors suggest that dependency grammar will play an increasingly important role as language processing systems seek to combine both structural and collocational information.

Acknowledgments

I am grateful to Fernando Pereira, Mike Riley, and Ido Dagan for valuable discussions on the issues addressed in this paper. Fernando Pereira and Ido Dagan also provided helpful comments on a draft of the paper.

References

H. Alshawi and D. Carter. Training and Scaling Preference Functions for Disambiguation. *Computational Linguistics*, 20: 635–648, 1994.

H. Alshawi, D. Carter, B. Gamback, and M. Rayner. Swedish-English QLF Translation. In H. Alshawi, editor, *The Core Language Engine*. Cambridge, Mass.: The MIT Press, 1992.

H. Alshawi and R. Crouch, Monotonic Semantic Interpretation. In *Proceedings of the 30th Annual Meeting of the Association for Computational Linguistics*, Newark, Del., 1992.

E. Brill. Automatic Grammar Induction and Parsing Free Text: A Transformation-Based Approach. In *Proceedings of the 31st Annual Meeting of the Association for Computational Linguistics*, pp. 259–265. Columbus, Ohio, 1993.

P. Brown, J. Cocke, S. Della Pietra, F. Jelinek V. Della Pietra, J. Lafferty, R. Mercer, and P. Rossin. A Statistical Approach to Machine Translation, *Computational Linguistics*, 16: 79–85, 1990.

J. Chang, Y. Luo, and K. Su. GPSM: A Generalized Probabilistic Semantic Model for Ambiguity Resolution. In *Proceedings of the 30th Annual Meeting of the Association for Computational Linguistics*, pp. 177–192. Newark, Del., 1992.

J. Chang and K. Su, A Corpus-Based Statistics-Oriented Transfer and Generation Model for Machine Translation. In *Proceedings of the 5th International Conference on Theoretical and Methodological Issues in Machine Translation,* Kyoto, Japan, 1993.

I. Dagan and A. Itai. Word Sense Disambiguation Using a Second Language Monolingual Corpus. *Computational Linguistics,* 20: 563–596, 1994.

I. Dagan, S. Marcus, and S. Markovitch. Contextual Word Similarity and Estimation from Sparse Data. In *Proceedings of the 31st Annual Meeting of the Association for Computational Linguistics,* pp. 164–171. Columbus, Ohio, 1993.

G. Gazdar, E. Klein, G. K. Pullum, and I. A. Sag. *Generalised Phrase Structure Grammar.* Oxford, Blackwell, 1985.

D. Hindle and M. Rooth. Structural Ambiguity and Lexical Relations, *Computational Linguistics,* 19: 103–120, 1993.

J. R. Hobbs, M. Stickel, P. Martin, and D. Edwards. Interpretation as Abduction. In *Proceedings of the 26th Annual Meeting of the Association for Computational Linguistics,* pp. 95–103. Buffalo, 1988.

R. A. Hudson, *Word Grammar.* Oxford, Blackwell, 1984.

P. Isabelle and E. Macklovitch, Transfer and MT Modularity. In *Proceedings of the 11th International Conference on Computational Linguistics,* pp. 115–117. Bonn, Germany, 1986.

F. Jelinek, R. L. Mercer, and S. Roukos. Principles of Lexical Language Modeling for Speech Recognition. In S. Furui and M. M. Sondhi, editors, *Advances in Speech Signal Processing.* New York, Marcel Dekker, 1992.

M. McCord. A Multi-Target Machine Translation System. In *Proceedings of the International Conference on Fifth Generation Computer Systems,* pp. 1141–1149. Tokyo, 1988.

C. S. Mellish. Implementing Systemic Classification by Unification. *Computational Linguistics,* 14: 40–51, 1988.

C. J. Pollard and I. A. Sag. *Information Based Syntax and Semantics: Volume I—Fundamentals.* Stanford, Calif., Center for the Study of Language and Information, 1987.

F. Pereira, N. Tishby, and L. Lee. Distributional Clustering of English Words. In *Proceedings of the 31st Annual Meeting of the Association for Computational Linguistics,* pp. 183–190. Columbus, Ohio, 1993.

M. Rayner and H. Alshawi. Deriving Database Queries from Logical Forms by Abductive Definition Expansion. In *Proceedings of the Third Conference on Applied Natural Language Processing.* Trent, Italy, 1992.

M. D. Richard and R. P. Lippmann. Neural Network Classifiers Estimate Bayesian *a posteriori* Probabilities. *Neural Computation,* 3: 461–483, 1991.

S. M. Shieber. *An Introduction to Unification-Based Approaches to Grammar.* Stanford, Calif., Center for the Study of Language and Information, 1986.

F. Smajda and K. McKeown. Automatically Extracting and Representing Collocations for Language Generation. In *Proceedings of the 28th Annual Meeting of the Association for Computational Linguistics*. Pittsburgh, 1990.

L. Taylor and C. Grover and E. J. Briscoe. The Syntactic Regularity of English Noun Phrases. In *Proceedings of the 4th European ACL Conference*. Manchester, England, pp. 256–263, 1989.

W. Weaver. Translation. In W. Locke and A. Booth, editors, *Machine Translation of Languages*. Cambridge, Mass., The MIT Press, 1955.

Chapter 3

Study and Implementation of Combined Techniques for Automatic Extraction of Terminology

Béatrice Daille

The acquisition of terminology for particular domains has long been a significant problem in natural language processing, requiring a great deal of manual effort. Statistical techniques hold out the promise of identifying likely candidates for domain-specific terminology, but analyzing word co-occurrences in text often uncovers collocations that are statistically significant but terminologically irrelevant—for example, frozen forms, collocations more characteristic of the language in general than the particular domain, and the like.

Assessing statistical significance is certainly part of the problem; for example, Dunning [1993] argues convincingly that many commonly used statistics, such as the χ^2 test, are based on assumptions that do not generally hold for text. One might conjecture, however, that the problem lies not only in the statistics per se, but in deciding what counts as a co-occurrence.

In her "Study and Implementation of Combined Techniques for Automatic Extraction of Terminology," Béatrice Daille takes this conjecture seriously, and explores a method in which the co-occurrences of interest are defined in terms of surface syntactic relationships rather than proximity of words or tags within a fixed window (compare with [Smadja, 1993], for example). She finds that filtering based on even shallow a priori linguistic knowledge proves useful; in addition, she investigates a number of alternative statistics (simple frequency, mutual information, likelihood ratio, etc.) in order to identify which of them is best for the purpose of identifying lexical patterns that constitute domain-specific terminology.

The approach to combining linguistic and statistical methods taken in Daille's work—using shallow syntactic relationships to define the co-occurrences over which statistical methods operate—is quite general, and has also proved useful in work other than terminology extraction, notably in word clustering and automatic thesaurus generation (e.g. [Grefenstette, 1994; Hindle, 1990; Pereira et al., 1993]; also see Hatzivassiloglou, chapter 4).—Eds.

1 Introduction

A terminology bank contains the vocabulary of a technical domain: terms, which refer to its concepts. Building a terminological bank requires a lot of time and both linguistic and technical knowledge. The issue at stake is the automatic extraction of terminology of a specific domain from a corpus. Current research on extracting terminology uses either linguistic specifications or statistical approaches. Concerning the former, [Bourigault, 1994] has proposed a program which extracts automatically from a corpus sequences of lexical units whose morphosyntax characterizes maximal technical noun phrases. This list of sequences is given to a terminologist to be checked. For the latter, several works ([Lafon, 1984; Church and Hanks, 1990; Calzolari and Bindi, 1990; Smadja and McKeown, 1990]) have shown that statistical scores are useful to extract collocations from corpora. The main problem with one or the other approach is the "noise": indeed, morphosyntactic criteria are not sufficient to isolate terms, and collocations extracted by statistical methods belong to various types of associations: functional, semantic, thematic, or uncharacterizable ones.

Our goal is to use statistical scores for extracting domain-specific collocations only and to forget about the other types of collocations. We proceed in two steps: first, by applying a linguistic filter which selects candidates from the corpus; then by applying statistical scores ranking these candidates and selecting the scores that fit our purpose best, in other words, scores that concentrate their high values to terms and their low values to co-occurrences that are not terms.

2 Linguistic Data

First, we study the linguistic specifications on the nature of terms in the technical domain of telecommunications for French. Then, taking into account these linguistics results, we present the method and the program that extract and count the candidate terms.

2.1 Linguistic Specifications

Terms are mainly multiword units of nominal type. They could be considered as a subclass of nominal compounds that inherit morphological and syntactic properties which have been stressed by studies on nominal compounding ([Gross et al., 1986; Noally, 1990], etc.). To be more precise, the structure of terms belongs to well-known morphosyntactic structures such as N ADJ, N_1 *de*

N_2, etc. and fits the general typology of French compounds elaborated by [Mathieu-Colas, 1988]. Some graphic indications (hyphen), morphological indications (restrictions in inflection), and syntactic ones (lack of article inside the structure) could also be good clues that a noun phrase is a term. [But these properties are not discriminatory contrary to the semantic property of terms: their referential monosemy.] A term is a label that refers to a concept, and in the best of all possible worlds, a term refers uniquely to one and only one concept within a given subject field, and this independently of its textual context. Terminologists, themselves agree that they encounter difficulty in defining exactly how to choose and delimit terms, since this semantic criterion relies mainly upon intuition. So, we have reinforced the criterion of unique referent with that of unique translation. A term as it refers to a unique and universal concept is ideally always translated by another such term in another language (though terms may have free or even contextually determined variants). We have manually extracted French terms, following these criteria from our bilingual corpus available in both French and English, the *Satellite Communication Handbook (SCH),* containing 200,000 words in each language. The translations of these terms mostly possess the morphosyntactic structures of English compounds too. Then, we classified terms according to their length; the *length* of a term is defined as the number of main items it contains.[1] From this classification, it appears that terms of length 2 are by far the most frequent ones. Because statistical methods demand a good representation in number of samples, we decided to extract in a first round only terms of length 2, which we will call *base-terms,* and which matched a list of previously determined patterns:

N ADJ *station terrienne (Earth station)*

N_1 *de* (DET) N_2 *zone de couverture (coverage zone)*

N_1 *à* (DET) N_2 *réflecteur à grille (grid reflector)*

N_1 PREP N_2 *liaison par satellite (satellite link)*

N_1 N_2 *diode tunnel (tunnel diode)*

Of course, terms exist whose length is greater than 2. But the majority of terms of length greater than 2 are created recurrently from base-terms. We have distinguished three operations that lead to a term of length 3 from a term of length 1 or

---

1. *Main items* are nouns, adjectives, adverbs, etc. Neither prepositions nor determiners are main items.

2: "overcomposition," modification, and coordination. We will illustrate these operations with a few examples where the base-terms appear inside brackets:

1. Overcomposition
   Two kinds of overcomposition have been pointed out: overcomposition by juxtaposition and overcomposition by substitution.
   (a) Juxtaposition
       A term obtained by juxtaposition is built with at least one base-term whose structure will not be altered. The example below illustrates the juxtaposition of a base-term and a simple noun:

       N_1 PREP$_1$ [N_2 PREP$_2$ N_3]

       modulation par [déplacement de phase] ([phase shift] keying)
   (b) Substitution
       Given a base-term, one of its main items is substituted by a base-term whose head is this main item. For example, in the N_1 PREP$_1$ N_2 structure, N_1 is substituted by a base-term of N_1 PREP$_2$ N_3 structure to create a term of N_1 PREP$_2$ N_3 PREP$_1$ N_2 structure:

       réseau à satellites + *réseau de transit* → *réseau de transit à satellites* (*satellite transit network*).

       We note in the above example that the structure of *réseau à satellites* (*satellite network*) is altered.

2. Modification
   Modifiers that could generate a new term from a base-term appear either inside or after it.
   (a) Insertion of modifiers
       Adjectives and adverbs are the current modifiers that could be inserted inside a base-term structure: adjectives in the N_1 PREP (DET) N_2 structure and adverbs in the N ADJ one: *liaisons* **multiples** *par satellite* (*multiple [satellite links]*) *réseaux* **entièrement** *numériques* (*all [digital networks]*)
   (b) Post-modification
       Adjectives and adverbial prepositional phrases of PREP ADJ N structure are the main modifiers that lead to the creation of new terms: post-adjectives can modify any kind of base-term; for example *[station terrienne] brouilleuse* (*interfering [earth(-)station]*). Adverbial prepositional phrases modify either simple nouns or base-terms[2]: *amplifica-*

---

2. In this case, the length of the term is equal to 4.

teur(s) [à faible bruit] ([low noise] amplifier(s)), [interface(s) usager-réseau] [à usage multiple] ([multipurpose] [user-network interface(s)]).

3. Coordination

Coordination is a rather complex syntactic phenomenon (term coordination has been studied in [Jacquemin, 1991]) and seldom generates new terms. Let us examine a rare example of a term of length 3 obtained by coordination:

N_1 *de* N_3 + N_2 *de* N_3 → N_1 *et* N_2 *de* N_3

assemblage de paquet + désassemblage de paquets → *assemblage et désassemblage de paquets (packet assembly/disassembly)*

It is difficult to determine whether a modified or overcomposed base-term is or is not a term. Take, for example, *bande latérale unique* (single sideband): *bande latérale* (*sideband*) is a base-term of structure N ADJ and *unique* (*single*) a very common post-modifier adjective in French. The fact that *bande latérale unique* is a term is indicated by the presence of the abbreviation *BLU* (*SSB*). As abbreviations are not introduced for all terms, the right way is surely to first extract base-terms, that is, *bande latérale* (*sideband*). Once you have base-terms, you can easily extract from the corpus terms of length greater than 2, at least post-modified base-terms and overcomposed base-terms by juxtaposition.

But, even if we have decided to extract only base-terms (length 2), we have to take into account their variations, or at least some of them. Variants of base-terms are classified under the following categories:

1. Graphic and orthographic variants

By graphic variants, we mean either the use or not of capitalized letters (*Service national* or *service national* (*(D/d)omestic service*)), or the presence or not of a hyphen inside the N_1 N_2 structure (*mode paquet* or *mode-paquet* (*packet (-)mode*)).

Orthographic variants concern N_1 PREP N_2 structure. For this structure, the number of N_2 is generally fixed, either singular or plural. However, we have encountered some exceptions: *réseau(x) à satellite, réseaux(x) à satellites* (*satellite network(s)*).

2. Morphosyntactic variants

Morphosyntactic variants refer to the presence or not of an article before the N_2 in the N_1 PREP N_2 structure: *ligne d'abonné, lignes de l'abonné* (*subscriber lines*), to the optional character of the preposition: *tension hélice, tension d'hélice* (*helix voltage*), and to synonymy relation between two base-terms of different structures: for example, N ADJ and N_1 *à* N_2: *réseau commuté, réseau à commutation (switched network)*.

3. Elliptical variants

A base-term of length 2 could be called up by an elliptical form: for example, *débit,* which is used instead of *débit binaire (bit rate)*.

After this linguistic investigation, we concentrate on terms of length 2 (base-terms) which seem by far the most frequent ones. Moreover, the majority of terms whose length is greater than 2 are built from base-terms. A statistical approach requires a good sampling, which base-terms provide. To filter base-terms from the corpus, we use their morphosyntactic structures. For this task, we need a tagged corpus where each item comes with its part of speech and its lemma. The part of speech is used to filter and the lemma to obtain an optimal sampling. We have used the stochastic tagger and the lemmatizer of the Scientific Center of IBM-France developed by the speech recognition team ([Dérouault, 1985; and El-Bèze, 1993]).

2.2 Linguistic Filters

We now face a choice: we can either isolate general collocations using statistics and then apply linguistic filters to retain only morphosyntactic sequences that characterize base-terms, or apply, first, linguistic filters, and then statistics. It is the latter strategy that has been adopted; indeed, the former has already been proposed by [Smadja, 1993] and does not seem adequate to take into account term variations. Indeed, computing statistics first involves collecting the possible collocates using a window of an arbitrary size. The size of the window is generally a compromise between a small or a large window: If you take a small window size, you miss many occurrences, mainly morphosyntactic variants as base-terms modified by several inserted modifiers, very frequent in French, and multiple coordinated base-terms; if you take a longer one, you obtain occurrences that do not refer to the same conceptual entity, many ill-formed sequences that do not characterizes terms, and, thus, wrong frequency counts may be. First, using linguistic filters based on part-of-speech tags appears to be the best solution. Moreover, as patterns that characterizes base-terms can be described by regular expressions, the use of finite automata seems a natural way to extract and count the occurrences of the candidate base-terms.

The frequency counts of the occurrences of the candidate terms are crucial as they are the parameters of the statistical scores. A wrong frequency count implies wrong or not relevant values of statistical scores. The objective is to optimize the count of base-term occurrences and to minimize the count of incorrect occurrences. Graphic, orthographic, and morphosyntactic variants of base-term (except synonymic variants) are taken into account as well as some syntactic variations that affect the base-term structure: coordination and insertion of modifiers. Coordination of two base-terms rarely leads to the creation of a new term of length greater than 2, so it is reasonable to think that the sequence *équipements de modulation et de démodulation* (*modulation and demodulation equipment*) is equivalent to the sequence *équipement de modulation et équipement de démodulation* (*modulation equipment and demodulation equipment*). Insertion of modifiers inside a base-term structure does not raise problems, except when this modifier is an adjective inserted inside an N_1 PREP N_2 structure. Let us examine the sequence *antenne parabolique de réception* (*parabolic receiving antenna*). This sequence could be a term of length 3 (obtained either by overcomposition or by modification) or a modified base-term, namely, *antenne de réception,* modified by the inserted adjective *parabolique*. On the one hand, we do not want to extract terms of length greater than 2, but on the other hand, it is not possible to ignore adjective insertion. So, we have chosen to accept insertion of the adjective inside N_1 PREP N_2 structure. This choice implies the extraction of terms of length 3 of N_1 ADJ PREP N_2 structure that are considered as terms of length 2. However, such cases are rare and the majority of N_1 ADJ PREP N_2 sequences refer to a N_1 PREP N_2 base-term modified by an adjective.

Each occurrence of a base-term is counted equally; we consider that there is equiprobability of the appearance of the term in the corpus. The occurrence of morphological sequences which characterize base-terms are classified under pairs: a pair is composed of two main items in a fixed order and collects all the sequences where the two lemmas of the pair appear in one of the allowed morphosyntactic patterns; for example, the sequence: *ligne d'abonné, lignes de l'abonné* (*subscriber lines*), and *ligne numérique d'abonné* (*digital subscriber line*) are each one occurrence of the pair (`ligne, abonné`). If we have the coordinated sequence *lignes et services d'abonné* (*subscriber lines and services*), we count one occurrence for the pair (`ligne, abonné`) and one occurrence for the pair (`service, abonné`). Our program scans the corpus and counts and extracts collocations whose syntax characterizes base-terms. Under each pair, we find all the different occurrences found with their frequencies and their location in the corpus (file, sentence, item). This program runs fast: for example, it took 2 minutes to extract 8,000 pairs from our corpus *SCH* (200,000 words) for the structure N_1 *prep* (DET) N_2 on a Sparc station ELC (SS1) under Sun-Os Release 4.1.3. Results presented in table 3.1 summarize

Table 3.1
Extraction results

Corpora	N ADJ	N_1 (prep(Det)) N_2
SCH		
1 occurrence	3,144	6,834
2 occurrences	655	1,503
> 2 occurrences	684	1,616
total	4,483	9,953
CBB		
1 occurrence	5,201	12,167
2 occurrences	1,507	3,481
>2 occurrences	2,113	6,288
total	8,821	21,936

the frequencies of co-occurrences expressed in terms of pairs extracted from two corpora, *SCH* and *CBB* (*Communication Blue Book*) (800,000 words).

In order to manually check if the candidate base-terms we have identified are indeed terms when seen in context, and that we have not missed any, we have developed a Shell program which inserts opening and closing brackets around the occurrences of the candidate pairs through the corpora. A sample of the CBB corpus where candidate pairs are bracketed is the following:

5828 22

on peut montrer que toute [2 [1 onde radioélectrique]1 à [3 polarisation]2 elliptique]3 peut être considére comme la somme de deux [4 composantes orthogonales]4 , par exemple de deux [6 [5 ondes à [7 polarisation]5 rectiligne]7 perpendiculaires]6 ou d'une [8 onde à [10 [9 polarisation]8 circulaire]9 lévogyre]10 et d'une [11 onde à [13 [12 polarisation]11 circulaire]12 dextrogyre]13 .

5828 23

une [2 [1 caractéristique importante]1 du [3 diagramme]2 de [4 rayonnement]3 d'une antenne]4 (notamment lorsque celle-ci est mise en oeuvre dans un [5 système de [6 réutilisation]5 des fréquences]6 [7 par double polarisation]7) est sa [8 pureté de polarisation]8 .

The brackets are indexed to determine the right opening and closing bracket of a candidate term; indeed, some candidate terms can also appear inside more complex candidate terms: in the above example, the N ADJ sequence (*onde radioélectrique*) inside the N_1 ADJ PREP N_2 (*onde radioélectrique à polarisation*) corresponds to a term of structure N_1 PREP N_2 (*onde à polarisation*) modified by the inserted adjective (*radioélectrique*). Twenty bracketed sentences taken at random have been checked and only two occurrences of a researched pattern were missing:

• The first miss belongs to the N ADJ pattern: the adjective *brouilleuse* appears inside parenthesis and is separated from the noun *composante* by another item itself inside parentheses: une [5 composante contrapolaire]5 (x) (brouilleuse),

• the second miss concerns also the N ADJ pattern: in the sequence: les polarisations quasi circulaires, the pair (*polarisation, circulaire*) is not recognized. This error comes from the tagger: indeed, the N ADJ finite-state machine asks for an agreement between the noun and the adjective and in this sequence, *polarisation* is well-tagged (feminine substantive in the plural inflection) but *circulaire* badly (adjective in the masculine and plural inflection). So, as there is no agreement between the adjective and the noun, this occurrence is not taken into account.

These misses show that:

1. It is not possible to encode in the finite-state machine all the marginal possible sequences where a candidate base-term appears.
2. The accuracy of this base-term extraction program relies upon the accuracy of the tagger.

Now that we have obtained a set of pairs, each pair representing a candidate base-term, we apply statistical scores to distinguish terms from non-terms among the candidates.

3 Lexical Statistics

The problem to solve now is to discover which statistical score is the best to isolate terms among our list of candidates. So, we compute several measures: frequencies, association criteria, Shannon diversity, and distance scores. All these measures could not be used for the same purpose: frequencies are the parameters of the association criteria, association criteria propose a conceptual sort of the pairs, and Shannon diversity and distance measures are not discriminatory scores but provide other types of information.

3.1 Frequencies and Association Criteria

From a statistical point of view, the two lemmas of a pair could be considered as two qualitative variables whose link has to be tested. A contingency table is defined for each pair (L_i, L_j):

	L_j	$L_{j'}$ with $j' \neq j$
L_i	a	b
$L_{i'}$ with $i' \neq i$	c	d

where:

a stands for the frequency of pairs involving both L_i and L_j,

b stands for the frequency of pairs involving L_i and $L_{j'}$,

c stands for the frequency of pairs involving $L_{i'}$ and L_j, and

d stands for the frequency of pairs involving $L_{i'}$ and $L_{j'}$.

The statistical literature proposes many scores which can be used to test the strength of the bond between the two variables of a contingency table. Some are well-known, such as the association ratio, close to the concept of mutual information introduced by [Church and Hanks, 1990]:

$$IM = \log_2 \frac{a}{(a + b)(a + c)} \tag{1}$$

the Φ^2 coefficient introduced by [Gale and Church, 1991]:

$$\Phi^2 = \frac{(ad - bc)^2}{(a + b)(a + c)(b + c)(b + d)}$$

or the Loglike coefficient introduced by [Dunning, 1993]:

$$\begin{aligned} Loglike = {} & a \log a + b \log b + c \log c + d \log d \\ & - (a + b) \log (a + b) - (a + c) \log (a + c) \\ & - (b + d) \log (b + d) - (c + d) \log (c + d) \\ & + (a + b + c + d) \log (a + b + c + d) \end{aligned} \tag{4}$$

A property of these scores is that their values increase with the strength of the bond of the lemmas. We have tried out several scores (more than 10) including IM, Φ^2, and Loglike, and we have sorted the pairs following the score value. Each score proposes a conceptual sort of the pairs. This sort, however, could put at the top of the list compounds that belong to general language rather than to the telecommunications domain. Since we want to obtain a list of telecommunication terms, it is essential to evaluate the correlation between the score values and the pairs and to find out which scores are the best to extract terminology. Therefore, we compared the values obtained for each score to a reference list of the domain. We obtained a list of over 6,000 French terms from EURODICAUTOM, the terminology data bank of the EEC, telecommunications section, which was developed by experts. We purchased the evaluation on 2,200 French pairs[3] of N_1 *de* (DET) N_2 structure, the most frequent and common French term structure, extracted from our corpus *SCH* (200,000 words). To limit the size of the reference list, we retained the intersection between our list of candidates and the EURODICAUTOM list, 1,200 pairs, thus getting rid of terms which we would not find in our corpus anyway, even if they belong to this technical domain. We assume that the reference list, 1,200 pairs of our list of 2,200 candidate pairs, is as complete as possible, so that base-terms that we might identify in our corpus are indeed found in the reference list. Each score yields a list where the candidates are sorted according to the decreasing score value. We have divided this list in equivalence classes which generally contain 50 successive pairs. The results of a score are represented graphically by a histogram in which the x-axis represents different classes, and the y-axis the ratio of good pairs. If all the pairs in a class belong to the reference list, we obtain the maximum ratio of 1; if none of the pairs appears in the reference list, the minimum ratio of 0 is reached. The ideal score should assign high (low) values to good (bad) pairs, that is, candidates which belong (which do not belong) to the reference list (in other words, the histogram of the ideal score should assign to equivalence classes containing the high (low) values of the score a ratio close to 1 [0]). We are not going to present here all the histograms obtained (see [Daille, 1994]). All of them show a general trend that confirms that the score values increase with the strength of the bond of the lemma. However, the growth is more or less clear, with more or less sharp variations. The most beautiful histogram is the simple frequency of the pair (see figure 3.1). This histogram shows that the more frequent the pair is, the more likely the pair is a term. Frequency is the most significant score for detecting terms of a technical domain. This result contradicts numerous results of lexical resources, which claim that association criteria are more significant than frequency: for example, all the most frequent pairs whose terminological status is undoubted share low values of association ratio [equation (1)], as, for example, *réseau à satellites* (*satellite network*) *IM* = 2.57,

---

3. Only pairs which appear at least twice in the corpus have been retained.

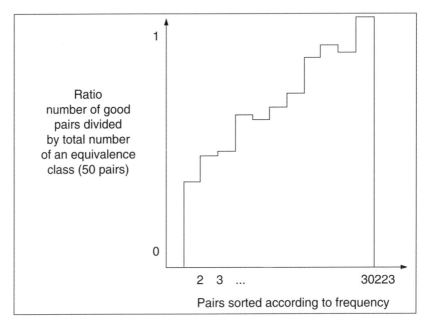

Figure 3.1
Frequency histogram.

liaison par satellite (*satellite link*) *IM* = 2.72, *circuit téléphonique* (*telephone circuit*) *IM* = 3.32, *station spatiale* (*space station*) *IM* = 1.17, etc. The remaining problem with the sort proposed by frequency is that it very quickly integrates bad candidates, that is, pairs which are not terms. So, we have preferred to elect the Loglike coefficient [equation (3)] the best score. Indeed, Loglike coefficient, which is a real statistical test, takes into account the pair frequency but accepts very little noise for high values. To give an element of comparison, the first bad candidate with frequency for the general pattern N_1 (PREP (DET)) N_2 is the pair (`cas, transmission`) which appears in 56th place; this pair, which is also the first bad candidate with Loglike, appears in 176th place. We give in table 3.2 the topmost 11 French pairs sorted by the Loglike coefficient (Logl) (Nbc is the number of the pair occurrences and IM the value of association ratio).

3.2 Diversity

Diversity, introduced by [Shannon, 1949], characterizes the marginal distribution of the lemma of a pair through the range of pairs. Its computation uses a

Table 3.2
Topmost pairs

Pairs of N_1 (PREP (DET)) N_2 structure	The most frequent pair sequence	Logl	Nbc	IM
(largeur, bande)	*largeur de bande* (197) (*bandwidth*)	1328	223	5.74
(température, bruit)	*température de bruit* 110 (*noise temperature*)	777	126	6.18
(bande, base)	*bande de base* (142) (*baseband*)	745	145	5.52
(amplificateur, puissance)	*amplificateur(s) de puissance* (137) (*power amplifier*)	728	137	5.66
(temps, propagation)	*temps de propagation* (93) (*propagation delay*)	612	94	6.69
(règlement, radiocommunication)	*règlement des radiocommunications* (60) (*radio regulation*)	521	60	8.14
(produit, intermodulation)	*produit(s) d'intermodulation* (61) (*intermoduation product*)	458	61	7.45
(taux, erreur)	*taux d'erreur* (70) (*error ratio*)	420	70	6.35
(mise, oeuvre)	*mise en oeuvre* (47) (*implementation*)	355	47	7.49
(télécommunication, satellite)	*télécommunication(s) par satellite* (88) (*satellite communication(s)*)	353	99	4.09
(bilan, liaison)	*bilan de liaison* (37) (*link budget*)	344	55	6.42

contingency table of length n: we give below as an example the contingency table that is associated with the pairs of the N ADJ structure:

$N_i Adj_j$	*progressif*	*porteur*	...	Total
onde	19	4	...	$nb_{(onde,.)}$
cornet	9	0	...	$nb_{(cornet,.)}$
...	...	...	...	...
Total	$nb_{(.,progressif)}$	$nb_{(.,porteur)}$	...	$nb_{(.,.)}$

The line counts $nb_{i.}$, which are found in the rightmost column, represent the distribution of the adjectives with regard to a given noun. The column counts $nb_{.j}$, which are found on the last line, represent the distribution of the nouns with regard to a given adjective. These distributions are called "marginal distributions" of the nouns and the adjectives for the N ADJ structure. Diversity is computed for each lemma appearing in a pair, using the formula:

$$H_i = nb_{i.} \log n_{i.} - \sum_{j=1}^{s} nb_{ij} \log nb_{ij}$$

$$H_j = nb_{.j} \log n_{.j} - \sum_{i=1}^{s} nb_{ij} \log nb_{ij}$$

(4)

For example, using the contingency table of the N ADJ structure above, diversity of the noun *onde* is equal to:

$$H_{(onde, .)} = nb_{(onde,.)} \log nb_{(onde,.)} - (nb_{(onde, progressif)} \log nb_{(onde, progressif)}$$
$$+ nb_{(onde, porteur)} \log nb_{(onde, porteur)} + ...)$$

We note H_1, diversity of the first lemma of a pair, and H_2, diversity of the second lemma. We take into account the diversity normalized by the number of occurrences of the pairs:

$$h_i = \frac{Hi}{n_{ij}}$$

$$h_j = \frac{Hj}{n_{ij}}$$

(5)

The normalized diversities h_1 and h_2 are defined from H_1 and H_2.

The normalized diversity provides interesting information about the distribution of the pair lemmas in the set of pairs. A lemma with a high diversity means that it appears in several pairs in equal proportion; conversely, a lemma that appears only in one pair owns a zero diversity (minimal value) and this whatever the frequency of the pair. High values of h_1 applied to the pairs of N ADJ structure characterizes nouns that could be seen as keywords of the domain: *réseau (network)*, *signal*, *antenne (antenna)*, *satellite*. Conversely, high values of h_2 applied to the pairs of N ADJ structure characterizes adjectives that do not take part in base-terms such as *nécessaire (necessary)*, *suivant (following)*, *important*, *différent (various)*, *tel (such)*, etc. The pairs with a zero diversity on one of their lemmas receive high values of association ratio and other association criteria and a nondefinite value of Loglike coefficient. However, the diversity is more precise because it indicates if the two lemmas appear only together as for (océan, indien) *(indian ocean)* ($H_1 = h_1 = H_2 = h_2 = 0$), or if not, which of the two lemmas appear only with the other, as for (réseau, maillé) (*mesh network*) ($H_2 = h_2 = 0$), where the adjective *maillé* appears only with *réseau* or for (codeur, idéal) (*ideal coder*) ($H_1 = h_1 = 0$) where the noun *codeur* appears only with the adjective *idéal*. Other examples are: (île, salomon) (*solomon island*), (hélium, gazeux) (*helium gas*), (suppresseur, écho) (*echo suppressor*). These pairs collect many frozen compounds and collocations of the current language. In future work, we will investigate how to incorporate the good results provided by diversity into an automatic extraction algorithm.

3.3 Distance Measures

French base-terms often accept modifications of their internal structure, as has been demonstrated previously. Each time an occurrence of a pair is extracted and counted, two distances are computed: the number of items, *Dist,* and the number of main items, *MDist,* which occur between the two lemmas. Then, for each pair, the mean and the variance of the number of items and main items are computed. The variance formula is:

$$V(X) = \frac{1}{n}\sum (x_i - \bar{x})^2$$

$$\sigma(X) = \sqrt{V(X)}$$

The distance measures bring interesting information concerning the morphosyntactic variations of the base-terms, but they do not allow making a decision on the status of term or non-term of a candidate. A pair that has no distance variation, whatever the distance, is or is not a term; we give now some examples of pairs which have no distance variations and which are not terms: *paire de signal* (*a pair of signal*), *type d'antenne* (*a type of antenna*), *organigramme de la figure* (*diagram of the figure*), etc. We illustrate below how the distance measures allow attributing to a pair its elementary type automatically, for example, either $N_1\,N_2$, N_1 PREP N_2, N_1 PREP DET N_2, or N_1 ADJ PREP (DET) N_2 for the general N_1 (PREP (DET)) N_2 structure.

1. Pairs with no distance variation $V(X) = 0$
   (a) $N_1\,N_2$: *Dist = 2 MDist = 2*
      - *liaison sémaphore, liaisons sémaphores* (*common signaling link(s)*)
      - *canal support, canaux support, canaux supports* (*bearer channel*)
   (b) N_1 PREP N_2: *Dist = 3 MDist = 2*
      - *accusé(s) de réception* (*acknowledgement of receipt*)
      - *refroidissement à air, refroidissement par air* (*cooling by air*)

  (c) $\mathbf{N}_1$ PREP DET $\mathbf{N}_2$: $Dist = 4\ MDist = 2$
- *sensibilité au bruit (susceptibility to noise)*
- *reconnaissance des signaux (signal recognition)*

  (d) $\mathbf{N}_1$ ADJ PREP $\mathbf{N}_2$: $Dist = 4\ MDist = 3$
- *réseau local de lignes, réseaux locaux de lignes (local line network(s))*
- *service fixe par satellite (fixed-satellite service)*

2. Pairs with distance variations $V(X) \neq 0$
- (liaison, satellite)

  liaison par satellite, liaisons par satellite

  liaisons (très rapides + numériques + téléphoniques nationales) par satellite

  liaisons numériques par satellites

  liaisons satellite

  liaisons entre satellites
- (ligne, abonné)

  ligne d'abonné, lignes d'abonné

  ligne de l'abonné, lignes de l'abonné

  ligne d'abonnés, lignes des abonnés

  ligne(s) (téléphonique(s) + numériques(s) + analogique(s)) d'abonné

  ligne(s) (numérique(s) + analogique(s)) de l'abonné

  lignes et services d'abonné

4 Conclusion

We have presented a combining approach for automatic term extraction. Starting from a first selection of lemma pairs representing candidate terms from a morphosyntactic point of view, we have applied and evaluated several statistical scores. The results were surprising: most association criteria (e.g., mutual association) did not give good results contrary to frequency. This bad behavior of the association criteria could be explained by the introduction of linguistic filters. We can note in any event that frequency undoubtedly characterizes terms, contrary to association criteria, which select in their high values frozen compounds belonging to general language. However, we preferred to elect the Loglike criterion rather than frequency as the best score. This latter takes into account the frequency of the pairs but provides a conceptual sort of high accuracy. Our system, which uses finite automata, allows us to increase the results of the extraction of lexical resources and to demonstrate the efficiency of incorporating linguistics in a statistical system. This method has been extended to bilingual terminology extraction using aligned corpora [Daille et al., 1994].

Acknowledgments

I thank the IBM-France team, and in particular Éric Gaussier and Jean-Marc Langé, for the tagged and lemmatized version of the French corpus and for their evaluation of statistics, and Owen Rambow for his review of the manuscript. Research was supported by the European Commission and IBM-France, through the *ET-10/63* project.

References

Didier Bourigault. *Acquisition de terminologie*. PhD thesis, EHESS, France, 1994.

Nicoletta Calzolari and Remo Bindi. Acquisition of lexical information from a large textual italian corpus. In *Proceedings of the Thirteenth International Conference on Computational Linguistics,* Helsinki, 1990.

Kenneth Ward Church and Patrick Hanks. Word association norms, mutual information, and lexicography. *Computational Linguistics,* 16(1): 22–29, 1990.

Béatrice Daille. *Approche mixte pour l'extraction automatique de terminologie: statistiques lexicales et filtres linguistiques*. PhD thesis, University of Paris 7, 1994.

Béatrice Daille, Éric Gaussier, and Jean-Marc Langé. Towards automatic extraction of monolingual and bilingual terminology. In *Proceedings of the Fifteenth International Conference on Computational Linguistics—COLING-94,* Kyoto, Japan, 1994.

Anne-Marie Dérouault. *Modélisation d'une langue naturelle pour la désambiguation des chaînes phonétiques*. PhD thesis, University of Paris VII, 1985.

Ted Dunning. Accurate methods for the statistics of surprise and coincidence. *Computational Linguistics,* 19(1): 61–76, 1993.

Marc El-Bèze. *Les Modèles de Langage Probabilistes: Quelques Domaines d'Applications*. PhD thesis, University of Paris-Nord, 1993. Habilitation à diriger les recherches [thesis required in France to be a professor].

William A. Gale and Kenneth W. Church. Concordances for parallel texts. In *Proceedings of the Seventh Annual Conference of the UW Centre for the New OED and Text Research, Using Corpora,* pp. 40–62, Oxford, 1991.

Gregory Grefenstette. *Explorations in Automatic Thesaurus Discovery*. Kluwer, 1994.

Gaston Gross, Jacques Chaurand, Robert Vivès, Michel Mathieu-Colas, and Pierre Billy. *Typologie des noms composés. Technical report, A.T.P.—Nouvelles recherches sur le langage,* University of Paris 13, Villetaneuse, 1986.

D. Hindle. Noun classification from predicate-argument structures. In *Proceedings of the 28th Annual Meeting of the Assocation of Computational Linguistics, Pittsburgh, Penna.,* pages 268–275, 1990. Association for Computational Linguistics, Morristown, NJ.

Christian Jacquemin. *Transformations des noms composés.* PhD thesis, University of Paris 7, 1991.

Pierre Lafon. *Dépouillements et Statistiques en Lexicométrie.* Geneva, Slatkine-Champion, 1984.

Michel Mathieu-Colas. *Typologie des noms composés. Technical Report 7, programme de recherches coordonées "informatique et linguistique,"* University of Paris 13, Paris, France, 1988.

Michèle Noally. *Le substantif épithète.* Paris, PUF, 1990.

Fernando Pereira, Naftali Tishby, and Lillian Lee. Distributional clustering of English words. In *Proceedings of the 31st Annual Meeting of the Association for Computational Linguistics,* June 1993.

C. E. Shannon, A Mathematical theory of communication. Urbana: University of Illinois Press, 1949.

Frank Smadja. Retrieving collocations from text: Xtract. *Computational Linguistics,* 19(1): 143–177, 1993.

Frank A. Smadja and Kathleen R. McKeown. Automatically extracting and representing collocations for language generation. In *Proceedings of the 28th Annual Meeting of the Association for Computational Linguistics,* pp. 252–259, 1990.

Chapter 4

Do We Need Linguistics When We Have Statistics? A Comparative Analysis of the Contributions of Linguistic Cues to a Statistical Word Grouping System

Vasileios Hatzivassiloglou

Is linguistic knowledge useful for a particular task, and what kinds of linguistic knowledge furnish the most benefit? Whether in the affirmative or in the negative, the answer to these questions often comes from a researcher's unsystematic past experience—or, equally often, from intellectual biases rather than careful exploration of the alternatives.

Hatzivassiloglou's chapter, "Do We Need Linguistics When We Have Statistics? A Comparative Analysis of the Contributions of Linguistic Cues to a Statistical Word Grouping System," represents an exemplary model of how such a careful exploration can be done. Like Daille (chapter 3) and others, Hatzivassiloglou adopts an approach in which linguistic knowledge is used to define the space of lexical co-occurrences, and then straightforward statistical methods are applied to the resulting co-occurrence frequencies. What distinguishes this work from most other efforts of this kind, however, is its attention to methodology: the variables of interest are carefully motivated and defined, a complete experimental design is used, and observed differences are evaluated in terms of statistical significance.

Moreover, Hatzivassiloglou explicitly considers the cost of incorporating linguistic knowledge into his system, both in development and on-line performance. Since the most successful combinations of linguistic and statistical approaches still rely on relatively shallow methods, this is an underappreciated topic; for real applications, deciding whether deeper linguistic analysis is worthwhile will require not only a rigorous analysis of performance, as illustrated here, but also a careful consideration of whether the benefits of added linguistic sophistication balance out the costs.—Eds.

1 Introduction

Historically, pure statistical, corpus-based approaches were among the first ones that were applied to natural language processing problems in general and lexical knowledge acquisition problems in particular. Such efforts took place very early: in the 1950s and early 1960s a considerable amount of research work was under way addressing problems such as machine translation and lexicon and thesaurus construction with purely statistical methods. However, the lack of sophisticated statistical models and powerful hardware led to rather disappointing results, and the statistical approach was largely abandoned in the 1970s in favor of knowledge-based, artificial intelligence (AI) approaches.

Yet, pure knowledge-based approaches, which use knowledge collected by human experts and entered in the system as an external source, also seem insufficient for providing an adequate solution to natural language problems. Such systems are effective when the domain and the vocabulary are tightly controlled, but fail to scale up in more general settings where knowledge acquisition becomes a major bottleneck. When this limitation of current knowledge-based systems became apparent, interest in statistical methods was renewed in the mid- and late 1980's, and continues unabated until now. This renaissance of statistical methods was particularly helped by recent successes of such "knowledge-poor" methods in problems such as part-of-speech tagging [Church, 1988; Kupiec, 1992; Cutting et al., 1992] and speech recognition [Waibel and Lee, 1990].

Once more, however, systems based on statistical methods alone have not been totally successful in solving most of the natural language processing problems they addressed. Consequently, a number of researchers have turned to combining linguistic, hand-encoded knowledge with statistical techniques as a means to improve overall performance, since it is reasonable to expect that the combined approach will potentially offer significantly better performance over either methodology alone. The interaction of statistical and linguistics-based components in a system is thus a topic of considerable current interest. However, when we consider such a hybrid system, several questions arise. Perhaps the most pressing ones are whether the linguistic knowledge actually helps in improving performance, and if so, whether the improvement is worth the effort needed to implement the linguistic modules and incorporate them in the system. In most cases answers to these questions, if supplied at all, are derived from intuitive beliefs and anecdotal evidence, rather than from a rigorous, quantitative comparison.

This chapter supplements these intuitive beliefs with actual evaluation data, obtained when several symbolic, linguistics-based modules were integrated in a statistical system. As the basis for our comparative analysis, we used a system we previously developed for the separation of adjectives into semantic groups [Hatzivassiloglou and McKeown, 1993]. We identified several different types of shallow linguistic knowledge that can be efficiently introduced into our system. We evaluated the system with and without each such feature, obtaining an estimate of each feature's positive or negative contribution to the overall performance. By matching cases where all system parameters are the same except for one feature, we assess the statistical significance of the differences found. Also, a statistical model of the system's performance in terms of the active features for each run offers a view of the contributions of features from a different angle, contrasting the significance of linguistic features (or other modeled system parameters) against one another.

Our analysis of the experimental results showed that many forms of linguistic knowledge make a significant positive contribution to the performance of the system. Other statistical systems that address word classification problems do not emphasize the use of linguistic knowledge and do not deal with a specific word class [Brown et al., 1992], or do not exploit as much linguistic knowledge as we do [Pereira et al., 1992]. As a result, a coarser classification is usually produced. In contrast, by limiting the system's input to adjectives, we can take advantage of specific syntactic relationships and additional filtering procedures that apply only to particular word classes. These sources of linguistic knowledge provide in turn the extra edge for discriminating among the adjectives at the semantic level.

In what follows, we briefly review our adjective grouping system, and discuss how the lexical semantic knowledge extracted by it can be used in a variety of natural language processing applications. We then present several different types of shallow linguistic knowledge that can be, and have been, efficiently introduced into this system. In section 6 we give the results of our evaluation of the system's performance on different combinations of features (linguistic modules) and analyze their statistical significance. We also estimate the relative importance of the linguistic modules and we measure the overall effect linguistic knowledge has in the word grouping system. We then proceed to discuss the cost of incorporating linguistic knowledge in the statistical system, and conclude by presenting arguments in favor of the relevance of these results to statistical approaches for other natural language processing problems.

2 Overview of the Adjective Grouping System

2.1 Definitions

Our adjective grouping system [Hatzivassiloglou and McKeown, 1993] starts with a set of adjectives to be clustered into groups of semantically related words. In linguistics, there is a long tradition of work associated with "semantic relatedness" and "groups of semantically related words." Trier [1934] proposed that the vocabulary of a natural language is organized in groups that he called *lexical fields* (*Wortfelder*), which represent *conceptual fields* (*Sinnfelder*), the latter being sets of closely related concepts. Trier's lexical fields closely correspond to the "groups of semantically related words" that our system aims to find. The work of Trier focused more on the diachronic and cross-linguistic aspect of lexical semantics, but a considerable number of linguists followed and extended his approach; see [Lehrer, 1974] for a comprehensive treatment of the theory of lexical and semantic fields. Unfortunately, the theory is mostly based on intuitive judgments; as Lyons [1977, p. 277] remarks,

What is lacking so far . . . is a more explicit formulation of the criteria which define a lexical field . . . The majority of lexical fields are not so neatly structured or as clearly separated as Trier originally suggested.

Given the lack of a formal definition of semantic groups, we will use an informal, intuitive definition for semantic relatedness, and treating semantic relatedness as an equivalence relation in the vocabulary, we will then define the semantic groups as the equivalence classes induced by this relation. What we mean by "semantically related" is that words belonging to the same group should consistently express a closeness in their meaning, for example, by being synonyms, antonyms, complementary terms, hyponyms, special cases of the same superordinate concept (co-hyponyms), or terms describing the same property. Informal criteria such as the above have been frequently used in linguistics. As in many cases where an informal definition is used, results based on this definition are open to criticism, such as the remarks by Lyons above, and there is disagreement on what exactly is the correct answer, given the same input. Correspondingly, there is difficulty in interpreting the results, and special care is needed during evaluation. Nevertheless, humans are able to judge the quality of semantic groupings, even if they frequently disagree and cannot fully externalize the criteria they use. Furthermore, groupings produced independently by several humans tend to agree to a degree that cannot be expected by chance, thus establishing that the organization of words into semantic classes is not arbitrary or artificial.

2.2 Algorithm and Implementation

Our system generally operates on a set of words from a particular syntactic class, using distributional criteria to measure the semantic similarity between these words. In other words, the semantic relatedness between words X and Y is measured on the basis of the similarity of the co-occurrence patterns of these words with words from other *informative* syntactic classes. The relevant classes of words are selected so that semantic constraints are expected to apply between them and the words from the original set that co-occur with them. In the version of the system used in the experiments described in this chapter, we group adjectives and we use nouns that are modified by the adjectives as this second informative syntactic class. We are currently extending the system to group nouns on the basis of co-occurring adjectives and verbs that participate in appropriate syntactic relationships with these nouns.

The system has access to a text corpus, which has been automatically tagged with part-of-speech information. All lexical semantic knowledge for the grouping task is extracted from the corpus; no semantic information about the adjectives or any other words is available to the system. The system operates by extracting modified nouns for each adjective, and, optionally, pairs of adjectives that we can expect to be semantically unrelated on linguistic grounds. The latter are adjectives that either modify the same noun in the same noun phrase (e.g., *big red truck*) or one of them modifies the other (e.g., *light blue scarf*); see [Hatzivassiloglou and McKeown, 1993] and especially [Hatzivassiloglou, 1995a] for a detailed analysis of this phenomenon. The estimated distribution of modified nouns for each adjective is represented as a vector, and a similarity score is assigned to each possible pair of adjectives. This is based on Kendall's τ, a nonparametric, robust estimator of correlation [Kendall, 1938, 1975].

Kendall's τ compares the two vectors by repeatedly comparing two pairs of their corresponding observations. Formally, if (X_i, Y_i) and (X_j, Y_j) are two pairs of frequencies for the adjectives X and Y that we are interested in grouping on the nouns i and j respectively, we call these pairs *concordant* if $X_i > X_j$ and $Y_i > Y_j$ or if $X_i < X_j$ and $Y_i < Y_j$. If $X_i > X_j$ but $Y_i < Y_j$, or if $X_i < X_j$ and $Y_i > Y_j$, the two pairs are *discordant*. In general, if the distributions of the two random variables X and Y across the various modified nouns are similar, we expect a large number of concordances, and consequently a small number of discordances since the total number of pairs of observations is fixed for the two variables. This is justified by the fact that a large number of concordances indicate that when one of the variables takes a "large" value the other also takes a "large" value on the corresponding observation; of course, "large" is a term that is interpreted in a relative manner for each variable.

Kendall's τ is defined as $p_c - p_d$, where p_c and p_d are the probabilities of observing a concordance or discordance respectively. It ranges from -1 to $+1$, with $+1$ indicating complete concordance, -1 complete discordance, and 0 (i.e., $p_c = p_d$) no correlation between X and Y. We use an unbiased estimator T for τ, which incorporates a correction for ties, that is, pairs of observations where $X_i = X_j$ or $Y_i = Y_j$ [Kendall, 1975, p. 75]. The estimator is also made asymmetric by ignoring observations for which the noun frequency is zero for both X and Y. For more details on the similarity measure and its advantages for our task, see [Hatzivassiloglou, 1995a].

Using the computed similarity scores and, optionally, the established relationships of non-relatedness, a nonhierarchical clustering method [Späth, 1985] assigns the adjectives to groups in a way that maximizes the within-group similarity (and therefore also maximizes the between-group dissimilarity). The system is given the number of groups to form as an input parameter.[1] The clustering algorithm operates in an iterative manner, starting from a random partition of the adjectives. An *objective function* Φ is used to score the current clustering. Each adjective is considered in turn and all possible moves of that adjective to another cluster are considered. The move that leads to the largest improvement in the value of Φ is executed, and the cycle continues through the set of words until no more improvements to the value of Φ are possible. Note that in this way a word may be moved several times before its final group is determined.

This is a hill-climbing method and therefore is guaranteed to converge in finite time, but it may lead to a local minimum of Φ, inferior to the global minimum that corresponds to the optimal solution. To alleviate this problem, the partitioning algorithm is called repeatedly[2] with different random starting partitions and the best solution produced from these runs is kept.

Figure 4.1 shows an example clustering produced by our system for one of the adjective sets analyzed in this chapter.

2.3 Evaluation

In many natural language processing applications, evaluation is performed either by using internal evaluation measures (such as perplexity [Brown et al.,

---

1. Determining this number from the data is probably the hardest problem in cluster analysis in general; see [Kaufman and Rousseeuw, 1990]. However, a reasonably good value for this parameter can be selected for our problem using heuristic methods.

2. In the current implementation, 50 times for each value of the number of clusters parameter.

1. deadly fatal	13. communist leftist
2. capitalist socialist	14. astonishing meager vigorous
3. clean dirty dumb	15. catastrophic disastrous harmful
4. hazardous toxic	16. dry exotic wet
5. insufficient scant	17. chaotic turbulent
6. generous outrageous unreasonable	18. confusing misleading
7. endless protracted	19. dismal gloomy
8. plain	20. dual multiple pleasant
9. hostile unfriendly	21. fat slim
10. delicate fragile unstable	22. affordable inexpensive
11. affluent impoverished prosperous	23. abrupt gradual stunning
12. brilliant clever energetic smart stupid	24. flexible lenient rigid strict stringent

Figure 4.1
Example clustering found by the system using all linguistic modules.

1992]) or by having human judges score the system's output. However, the first approach produces results that depend on the adopted model, while the second approach frequently introduces bias and inflation of the scores, especially when the "correct" answer is not well defined (as is the case with most natural language processing problems). To address these deficiencies of traditional evaluation approaches, we employ model solutions constructed by humans independently of the system's proposed solution. The humans receive the list of adjectives that are to be clustered, a description of the domain, and general instructions about the task. To avoid introducing bias in the evaluation, the instructions do not include low-level details such as the number of clusters or specific tests for deciding whether any two words should be in the same group.

In order to compare two partitions of the same set of words, we convert each partition to a list of "yes/no" decisions as follows: We view each possible pair of the words in the set as a decision point, with a "yes" answer in the current partition if the two adjectives are placed in the same group and a "no" answer otherwise. Then, we can apply the standard information retrieval measures precision and recall [Frakes and Baeza-Yates, 1992] to measure how close any two such lists of decisions are, or more precisely, how similar one such list is to another which is considered as the reference model. Considering the answers in the reference list as the correct ones, *precision* is defined as the percentage of correct "yes" answers reported in the list that is evaluated over the total number of "yes" answers in that list. Similarly, *recall* is defined as the percentage of correct "yes" answers in the tested list over the total number of (by definition, correct) "yes" answers in the reference list.

The two evaluation measures defined above rate complementary aspects of the correctness of the evaluated partition. In order to perform comparisons between different variants of the grouping system, corresponding to the use of different combinations of linguistic modules, we need to convert this pair of scores to a single number. For this purpose we use the F-measure score [Van Rijsbergen, 1979], which produces a number between precision and recall that is larger when the two measures are close together, and thus favors partitions that are balanced in the two types of errors (false positives and false negatives). Placing equal weight on precision and recall, the *F-measure* is defined as

$$\text{F-measure} = \frac{2 \cdot \text{precision} \cdot \text{recall}}{\text{precision} + \text{recall}}$$

Up to this point, we have considered comparisons of one partition of words against another such partition. However, given the considerable disagreement that exists between groupings of the same set of words produced by different humans, we decided to incorporate multiple models in the evaluation. Previously, multiple models have been used indirectly to construct a single "best" or most representative model, which is then used in the evaluation [Gale et al., 1992a; Passonneau and Litman, 1993]. Although this approach reduces the problems caused by relying on a single model, it does not allow the differences between the models to be reflected in the evaluation scores. Consequently, we developed an evaluation method that *simultaneously* uses multiple models, directly reflects the degree of disagreement between the models in the produced scores, and automatically weighs the importance of each decision point according to the homogeneity of the answers for it in the multiple models. We have extended the information retrieval measures of precision, recall, fallout, and F-measure for this purpose; the mathematical formulation of the generalized measures is given in [Hatzivassiloglou and McKeown, 1993] and [Hatzivassiloglou, 1995a].

In the experiments reported in this chapter, we employ eight or nine human-constructed models for each adjective set. We base our comparisons on and report the generalized F-measure scores. In addition, since the correct number of groupings is something that the system cannot yet determine (and, incidentally, something that human evaluators disagree about), we run the system for the five cases in the range -2 to +2 around the average number of clusters employed by the humans and average the results. This smoothing operation prevents an accidental high or low score being reported when a small variation in the number of clusters produces very different scores.

It should be noted here that the scores reported should not be interpreted as linear percentages. The problem of interpreting the scores is exacerbated in our context because of the structural constraints imposed by the clustering and the presence of multiple models. Even the best clustering that could be produced would not receive a score of 100, because of the disagreement among humans on what is the correct answer; applying the same evaluation method to score each model constructed by humans for the three adjective sets used in this comparative study against the other human-constructed models leads to an average score of 60.44 for the human evaluators. To clarify the meaning of the scores, we accompany them with lower and upper bounds for each adjective set we examine. These bounds are obtained by the performance of a system that creates random groupings (averaged over many runs) and by the average score of the human-produced partitions when evaluated against the other human-produced models respectively.

3   Motivation

3.1   Applications

The output of the word grouping system that we described in the previous section is used as the basis for the further processing of the retrieved groups: the classification of groups into scalar and nonscalar ones, the identification of synonyms and antonyms within each semantic group, the labeling of words as positive or negative within a scale, and the ordering of scalar terms according to semantic strength. In this way, the grouping system is used as the first part of a larger system for corpus-based computational lexicography, which in turn produces information useful for a variety of natural language processing applications. We briefly list below some of these applications:

• The organization of words into semantic groups can be exploited in statistical language modeling, by pooling together the estimates for the various words in each group [Sadler, 1989; Hindle, 1990; Brown et al., 1992]. This approach significantly reduces the sparseness of the data, especially for low-frequency words.
• A study of medical case histories and reports has shown that frequently physicians use multiple modifiers for the same term that are incompatible (e.g., they are synonyms, contradict each other, or one represents a specialized case of the other) [Moore, 1993]. Given the technical character of these words, it is

quite hard for non-specialists to edit these incorrect expressions, even to identify such problematic cases. But the output of the word grouping system, which identifies semantically related words, can be used to flag occurrences of incompatible modifiers.

• Knowledge of the synonyms and antonyms of particular words can be used during both understanding and generation of text. Such knowledge can help with the handling of unknown words during understanding and increase the paraphrasing power of a generation system.

• Knowledge of semantic polarity (positive or negative status with respect to a norm) can be combined with corpus-based collocation extraction tools [Smadja, 1993] to automatically produce entries for the *lexical functions* used in Meaning-Text Theory for text generation [Mel'čuk and Pertsov, 1987]. For example, if the collocation extraction tool identifies the phrase *hearty eater* as a recurrent one, then knowing that *hearty* is a positive term enables the assignment of *hearty* to the lexical function MAGN (standing for *magnify*), that is, MAGN(*eater*) = *hearty*.

• The relative semantic strength of scalar adjectives directly correlates with the *argumentative force* of the adjectives in the text. Consequently, the relative semantic strength information can be used in language understanding to properly interpret the meaning of scalar words and in generation to select the appropriate word to lexicalize a semantic concept with the desired argumentative force [Elhadad, 1991].

• Scalar words obey pragmatic constraints, for example, scalar implicature [Levinson, 1983; Hirshberg, 1985]. If the position of the word on the scale is known, the system can draw the implied pragmatic inferences during text analysis, or use them for appropriate lexical choice decisions during generation. In particular, such information can be used for the proper analysis and generation of negative expressions. For example, *not hot* usually means *warm,* but *not warm* usually means *cold.*

3.2   The Need for Automatic Methods for Word Grouping

In recent years, the importance of lexical semantic knowledge for language processing has become recognized. Some of the latest dictionaries designed for human use include explicit lexical semantic links; for example, the COBUILD dictionary [Sinclair, 1987] explicitly lists synonyms, antonyms, and superordinates for many word entries. WordNet [Miller et al., 1990] is perhaps the best-known example of a large lexical database compiled by lexicographers specifically for computational applications, and it has been used in several natural language systems (e.g., [Resnik, 1993; Resnik and Hearst, 1993; Knight and Luk, 1994; Basili et al., 1994]). Yet, WordNet and the machine-readable versions of dictionaries and theusari still suffer from a number of disadvantages when compared with the alternative of an automatic, corpus-based approach:

• All entries must be encoded by hand, which represents significant manual effort.

• Changes to lexical entries may necessitate the careful examination and potential revision of other related entries to maintain the consistency of the database.

• Many types of lexical semantic knowledge are not present in current dictionaries or in WordNet. Most dictionaries emphasize the syntactic features of words, such as part of speech, number, and form of complement. Even when dictionary designers try to focus on the semantic component of lexical knowledge, the results have not yet been fully satisfactory. For example, neither COBUILD nor WordNet includes information about scalar semantic strength.

• The lexical information is not specific to any domain. Rather, the entries attempt to capture what applies to the language at large, or represent specialized senses in a disjunctive manner. Note that semantic lexical knowledge is most sensitive to domain changes. Unlike syntactic constraints, semantic features tend to change as the word is used in a different way in different domains. For example, our word grouping system identified *preferred* as the word most closely semantically related to *common;* this association may seem peculiar at first glance, but is indeed a correct one for the domain of stock market reports and financial information from which the training material was collected.

• Time-varying information, that is, the currency of words, compounds, and collocations, is not adjusted automatically.

• The validity of any particular entry depends on the assumptions made by the particular lexicographer(s) who compiled that entry. In contrast, an automatic system can be more thorough and impartial, since it bases its decisions on actual examples drawn from the corpus.

An automatic corpus-based system for lexical knowledge extraction such as our word grouping system offsets these disadvantages of static human-constructed knowledge bases by automatically adapting to the domain sublanguage. Its disadvantage is that while it offers potentially higher recall, it is generally less precise than knowledge bases carefully constructed by human lexicographers. This disadvantage can be alleviated if the output of the automatic system is modified by human experts in a post-editing phase.

4   Linguistic Features and Alternative Values for Them

We have identified several sources of symbolic, linguistic knowledge that can be incorporated in the word grouping system, augmenting the basic statistical component. Each such source represents a parameter of the system, that is, a feature that can be present or absent or more generally take a value from a pre-defined set. In this section we present first one of these parameters that can take several values, namely the method of extracting data from the corpus, and then several other binary-valued features.

4.1   Extracting Data from the Corpus

When the word-clustering system partitions adjectives in groups of semanti-cally related ones, it determines the distribution of related (modified) nouns for each adjective and eventually the similarity between adjectives from pairs of the form (adjective, modified noun) that have been observed in the corpus. Direct information about semantically unrelated adjectives (in the form of appropriate adjective-adjective pairs) can also be collected from the corpus. Therefore, a first parameter of the system and a possible dimension for com-parisons is the method employed to identify such pairs in free text.

There are several alternative models for this task of data collection, with dif-ferent degrees of linguistic sophistication. A first model is to use no linguistic knowledge at all[3]: we collect for each adjective of interest all words that fall within a window of some predetermined size. Naturally, no negative data (adjective-adjective pairs) can be collected with this method. However, the method can be implemented easily and does not require the identification of any linguistic constraints so it is completely general. It has been used for diverse problems such as machine translation and sense disambiguation [Gale et al., 1992b; Schütze, 1992].

A second model is to restrict the words collected to the same sentence as the adjective of interest and to the word class(es) that we expect on linguistic grounds to be relevant to adjectives. For our application, we collect all nouns in the vicinity of an adjective without leaving the current sentence. We assume that these nouns have some relationship with the adjective and that semanti-cally different adjectives will exhibit different collections of such nouns. This model requires only part-of-speech information (to identify nouns) and a method of detecting sentence boundaries. It uses a window of fixed length to

---

3. Aside from the concept of a word, which is usually approximated by defining any string of characters separated by white space or punctuation marks as a word.

define the neighborhood of each adjective. Again, negative knowledge such as pairs of semantically unrelated adjectives cannot be collected with this model. Nevertheless, it has also been widely used, for example, for collocation extraction [Smadja, 1993] and sense disambiguation [Liddy and Paik, 1992].

Since we are interested in nouns modified by adjectives, a third model is to collect a noun immediately following an adjective, assuming that this implies a modification relationship. Pairs of consecutive adjectives, which are necessarily semantically unrelated, can also be collected.

Up to this point we have successively restricted the collected pairs on linguistic grounds, so that less but more accurate data are collected. For the fourth model, we extend the simple rule given above, using linguistic information to catch more valid pairs without sacrificing accuracy. We employ a pattern matcher that retrieves any sequence of one or more adjectives followed by any sequence of zero or more nouns. These sequences are then analyzed with heuristics based on linguistics to obtain pairs.

The regular expression and pattern matching rules of the previous model can be extended further, forming a grammar for the constructs of interest. This approach can detect more pairs, and at the same time address known problematic cases not detected by the previous models.

We implemented the above five data extraction models, using typical window sizes for the first two methods (50 and 5 on each side of the window respectively) which have been found appropriate for other problems before. Unfortunately, the first model proved to be excessively demanding in resources for our comparative experiments,[4] so we dropped it from further consideration and use the second model as the baseline of minimal linguistic knowledge. For the fifth model, we developed a finite-state grammar for noun phrases which is able to handle both predicative and attributive modification of nouns, conjunctions of adjectives, adverbial modification of adjectives, quantifiers, and apposition of adjectives to nouns or other adjectives.[5] A detailed description of this grammar and its implementation can be found in [Hatzivassiloglou, 1995b].

4.2 Other Linguistic Features

In addition to the data extraction method, we identified three other areas where linguistic knowledge can be introduced in our system. First, we can employ

4. For example, 12,287,320 word pairs in a 151 MB file were extracted for the 21 adjectives in our smallest test set. Other researchers have also reported similar problems of excessive resource demands with this "collect all neighbors" model [Gale et al., 1992b].
5. For efficiency reasons we did not consider a more powerful formalism.

morphology to convert plural nouns to the corresponding singular ones and adjectives in comparative or superlative degree to their base form. This conversion combines counts of similar pairs, thus raising the expected and estimated frequencies of each pair in any statistical model.

Another potential application of symbolic knowledge is the use of a spell-checking procedure to eliminate typographical errors from the corpus. We implemented this component using the UNIX *spell* program and associated word list, with extensions for hyphenated compounds. Unfortunately, since a fixed and domain-independent word list is used for this process, some valid but overspecialized words may be discarded too.

Finally, we have identified several potential sources of additional knowledge that can be extracted from the corpus (e.g., conjunctions of adjectives) and can supplement the primary similarity relationships. In this comparison study we implemented and considered the significance of one of these knowledge sources, namely the negative examples offered by adjective-adjective pairs where the two adjectives have been observed in a syntactic relationship that strongly indicates semantic unrelatedness.

5   The Comparison Experiments

In the previous section we identified four parameters of the system, the effects of which we want to analyze. But in addition to these parameters, which can be directly varied and have predetermined possible values, several other variables can affect the performance of the system.

First, the performance of the system depends naturally on the adjective set that is to be clustered. Presumably, variations in the adjective set can be modeled by several parameters, such as the size of the set, the number of semantic groups in it, and the strength of semantic relatedness among its members, plus several parameters describing the properties of the adjectives in the set in isolation, such as frequency, specificity, etc.

A second variable that affects the clustering is the corpus that is used as the main knowledge source, through the observed co-occurrence patterns. Again the effects of different corpora can be separated into several factors, for example, the size of the corpus, its generality, the genre of the texts, etc.

Since in these experiments we are interested in quantifying the effect of the linguistic knowledge in the system, or more precisely of the linguistic knowledge that we can explicitly control through the four parameters discussed above, we did not attempt to model in detail the various factors entering the system as a result of the choice of adjective set and corpus. However, we are interested in measuring the effects of the linguistic parameters in a wide range of contexts. Therefore, we included in our experiment model two additional parameters, representing the corpus and the adjective set used.

We used the 1987 *Wall Street Journal* articles from the ACL-DCI (Association for Computational Linguistics–Data Collection Initiative) as our corpus. We selected four subcorpora to study the relationship of corpus size with linguistic feature effects: subcorpora of 330,000 words, 1 million words, 7 million words, and 21 million words (the last consisting of the entire 1987 corpus) were selected as representative. Each selected subcorpus contained the selected subcorpora of smaller sizes, and was constructed by sampling across the whole range of the entire corpus at regular intervals. Since we use subsets of the same corpus, we are essentially modeling the corpus size parameter only.

For each corpus, we analyzed three different sets of adjectives, listed in figures 4.2, 4.3, and 4.4. The first of these adjective test sets was selected from a similar corpus, contains 21 words of varying frequencies that all associate strongly with a particular noun (*problem*), and was analyzed in [Hatzivassiloglou and McKeown, 1993]. The second set (43 adjectives) was selected with the constraint that it contain high-frequency adjectives (more than 1000 occurrences in the 21-million-word corpus). The third set (62 adjectives) satisfies the opposite constraint, containing adjectives of relatively low frequency (between 50 and 250). Figure 4.1 on page 73 shows a typical grouping found by our system for the third set of adjectives, when the entire corpus and all linguistic modules were used.

These three sets of adjectives represent various characteristics of the adjective sets that the system may be called on to cluster. First, they explicitly represent increasing sizes of the grouping problem. The second and third sets also contrast the independent frequencies of their member adjectives. Furthermore, the less frequent adjectives of the third set tend to be more specific than the more frequent ones. The human evaluators reported that the task of classification was

antitrust	international	old	staggering
big	legal	political	technical
economic	little	potential	unexpected
financial	major	real	
foreign	mechanical	serious	
global	new	severe	

Figure 4.2
Test set 1: Adjectives strongly associated with the word *problem*.

annual	hard	negative	public
big	high	net	quarterly
chief	important	new	recent
commercial	initial	next	regional
current	international	old	senior
daily	likely	past	significant
different	local	positive	similar
difficult	low	possible	small
easy	military	pre-tax	strong
final	modest	previous	weak
future	national	private	

Figure 4.3
Test set 2: High-frequency adjectives.

abrupt	dismal	hostile	slim
affluent	dry	impoverished	smart
affordable	dual	inexpensive	socialist
astonishing	dumb	insufficient	strict
brilliant	endless	leftist	stringent
capitalist	energetic	lenient	stunning
catastrophic	exotic	meager	stupid
chaotic	fat	misleading	toxic
clean	fatal	multiple	turbulent
clever	flexible	outrageous	unfriendly
communist	fragile	plain	unreasonable
confusing	generous	pleasant	unstable
deadly	gloomy	prosperous	vigorous
delicate	gradual	protracted	wet
dirty	harmful	rigid	
disastrous	hazardous	scant	

Figure 4.4
Test set 3: Low- to medium-frequency adjectives.

easier for the third set, and their models exhibited about the same degree of agreement for the second and third sets, although the third set is significantly larger.

By including the parameters "corpus size" and "adjective set," we have six parameters that we can vary in the experiments. Any remaining factors affecting the performance of the system are modeled as random noise,[6] so statistical methods are used to evaluate the effects of the selected parameters. The six chosen parameters are completely orthogonal, with the exception that parameter "negative knowledge" must have the value "not used" when parameter "extraction model" has the value "nouns in vicinity." In order to avoid introducing imbalance in the experiment, we constructed a complete designed experiment [Hicks, 1982] for all their $(4 \times 2 - 1) \times 2 \times 2 \times 4 \times 3 = 336$ valid combinations.[7]

6   Experimental Results

6.1   Average Effect of Each Linguistic Parameter

Presenting the scores obtained in each of the 336 individual experiments performed, which correspond to all valid combinations of the six modeled parameters, is both too demanding in space and not especially illuminating. Instead, we present several summary measures. We measured the effect of each particular setting of each linguistic parameter of section 4 by averaging the scores obtained in all experiments where that particular parameter had that particular value. In this way, table 4.1 summarizes the differences in the performance of the system caused by each parameter. Because of the complete design of the experiment, each value in table 4.1 is obtained in runs that are identical to the runs used for estimating the other values of the same parameter except for the difference in the parameter itself.[8]

Table 4.1 shows that there is indeed improvement with the introduction of any of the proposed linguistic features, or with the use of a linguistically more sophisticated extraction model. To assess the statistical significance of these differences, we compared each run for a particular value of a parameter with

6. Including some limited in extent but truly random effects from our nondeterministic clustering algorithm.

7. Recall that a designed experiment is *complete* when at least one trial, or *run*, is performed for every valid combination of the modeled predictors.

8. The slight asymmetry in parameters "extraction model" and "negative knowledge" is accounted for by leaving out non-matching runs.

Table 4.1
Average F-measure scores for each value of each linguistic feature

Parameter	Value	Average score
Extraction model	Parsing	30.29
	Pattern matching	28.88
	Observed pairs	27.87
	Nouns in vicinity	22.36
Morphology	Yes	28.60
	No	27.53
Spell-checking	Yes	28.12
	No	28.00
Use of negative knowledge	Yes	29.40
	No	28.63

the corresponding identical (except for that parameter) run for a different value of the parameter. Each pair of values for a parameter produces in this way a set of paired observations. On each of these sets, we performed a sign test [Gibbons and Chakraborti, 1992] of the null hypothesis that there is no real difference in the system's performance between the two values, that is, that any observed difference is due to chance. We counted the number of times that the first of the two compared values led to superior performance relative to the second, distributing ties equally between the two cases as is the standard practice in classifier induction and evaluation. Under the null hypothesis, the number of times that the first value performs better follows the binomial distribution with parameter $p = 0.5$. Table 4.2 gives the results of these tests along with the probabilities that the same or more extreme results would be encountered by chance. We can see from the table that all types of linguistic knowledge except spell-checking have a beneficial effect that is statistically significant at, or below, the 0.1% level.

6.2   Comparison Among Linguistic Features

In order to measure the significance of the contribution of each linguistic feature relative to the other linguistic features, we fitted a linear regression model [Draper and Smith, 1981] to the data. We use the six parameters of the experiments as the predictors, and the F-measure score of the corresponding clustering[9]

---

9. Averaged over five adjacent values of the number of clusters parameter, as explained in section 2.3.

Table 4.2
Statistical analysis of the difference in performance offered by each linguistic feature

Parameter tested	Test		Comparisons	First value better than second	Probability
	First value	Second value			
Extraction model	Parsing	Pattern matching	96	64	0.0014
	Parsing	Observed pairs	96	66	0.0003
	Parsing	Nouns in vicinity	48	42	10^{-7}
	Pattern matching	Observed pairs	96	61	0.0104
	Pattern matching	Nouns in vicinity	48	41	$6.24 \cdot 10^{-7}$
	Observed pairs	Nouns in vicinity	48	36	0.0007
Morphology	Used	Not used	168	107	0.0005
Spell-checking	Used	Not used	168	94	0.1425
Negative knowledge	Used	Not used	144	97	$3.76 \cdot 10^{-5}$

The rightmost column gives the probability that the same or more extreme results would have been obtained if a change between the two contrasted parameter values had no effect on system performance.

as the response variable. In such a model the response R is assumed to be a linear function (weighted sum) of the predictors V_i, that is,

$$R = \beta_0 + \sum_{i=1}^{n} \beta_i V_i \qquad (1)$$

where V_i is the i-th predictor and β_i is its corresponding weight. Table 4.3 shows the weights found by the fitting process for the experimental data collected for all valid combinations of the six parameters that we model. These weights indicate by their absolute magnitude and sign how important each predictor is and whether it contributes positively or negatively to the final result. Numerical values such as the corpus size enter equation (1) directly as predictors, so table 4.3 indicates that each additional million words of training text

Table 4.3
Fitted coefficients for the linear regression model that contrasts the effects of various parameters in overall system performance

Variable	Weight
Intercept	18.7997
Corpus size (in millions of words)	0.9417
Extraction method (pairs vs. nouns in vicinity)	5.1307
Extraction method (sequences vs. nouns in vicinity)	6.1418
Extraction method (parser vs. nouns in vicinity)	7.5423
Morphology	0.5371
Spell-checking	0.0589
Adjective set (2 vs. 1)	2.5996
Adjective set (3 vs. 1)	-11.4882
Use of negative knowledge	0.3838

increases the performance of the system by 0.9417 on average. For binary features, the weights in table 4.3 indicate the increase in the system's performance when the feature is present, so the introduction of morphology improves the system's performance by 0.5371 on average. The different possible values of the categorical variables "adjective set" and "extraction model" are encoded as contrasts with a base case; the weights associated with each such value show the change in score for the indicated value in contrast to the base case (adjective set 1 and the minimal linguistic knowledge represented by extraction model "nouns in vicinity," respectively). For example, using the finite-state parser instead of the "nouns in vicinity" model improves the score by 7.5423 on average, while going from adjective set 2 to adjective set 3 decreases the score by $-(-2.5996 - 11.4882) = 14.0878$ on average. Finally the intercept β_0 gives a baseline performance of a minimal system that uses the base case for each parameter; the effects of corpus size are to be added to this system.

From table 4.3 we can see that the data extraction model has a significant effect on the quality of the produced clustering, and among the linguistic parameters is the most important one. Increasing the size of the corpus also significantly increases the score. The adjective set that is clustered also has a major influence on the score, with rarer adjectives leading to worse clusterings. Note, however, that these are average effects, taken over a wide range of different settings for the system. In particular, while the system produces bad partitions for adjective set 3 when the corpus is small, when the largest corpus (21 million words) is used the partitions produced for test set 3 are equal in quality or better than the partitions produced for the other two sets with the same corpus. The two linguistic features "morphology" and "negative knowledge" have less pronounced although still significant effects, while spell-checking offers minimal improvement that probably does not justify the effort of implementing the module and the cost of activating it at run-time.

6.3   Overall Effect of Linguistic Knowledge

Up to this point we have described averages of scores or of score differences, taken over many combinations of features that are orthogonal to the one studied. These averages are good for establishing the *existence* of a performance difference caused by the different values of each feature, across all possible combinations of the other features. They are not, however, representative of the performance of the system in a particular setting of parameters, nor are they suitable for describing the difference between features quantitatively, since they are averages taken over widely differing settings of the system's parameters. In particular, the inclusion of very small corpora drives the average scores down, as we have confirmed by computing averages separately for each value of the corpus size parameter. To give a feeling of how important the introduction of linguistic knowledge is *quantitatively,* we compare in table 4.4 the

Table 4.4
Overall effect of linguistic knowledge in the evaluation score

	Adjective set 1	Adjective set 2	Adjective set 3
Random partitions	9.66 (17.90%)	6.21 (9.66%)	3.80 (6.03%)
No linguistic components active	24.51 (45.41%)	38.51 (59.92%)	33.21 (52.66%)
All linguistic components active	39.06 (72.36%)	44.73 (69.60%)	46.17 (73.20%)
Humans	53.98	64.27	63.07

Two versions of the system (with all or none of the linguistic modules active) are contrasted with the performance of a random classifier and that of the humans. The scores were obtained on the 21-million-word corpus, using a smoothing window of three adjacent values of the number of clusters parameter centered at the average value for that parameter in the human-prepared models. We also show the percentage of the score of the humans that is attained by the random classifier and each version of the system.

results obtained with the full corpus of 21 million words for the two cases of having all or none of the linguistic components active. The scores obtained by a random system that produces partitions of the adjectives with no knowledge except the number of groups are included as a lower bound. These estimates are obtained after averaging the scores of 20,000 such random partitions for each adjective set. The average scores that each human model receives when compared with all other human models are also included, as an estimate of the maximum score that can be achieved by the system. That maximum depends on the disagreement between models for each adjective set. For these measurements we use a smaller smoothing window of size 3 instead of 5, which is fairer to the system when its performance is compared with the humans. We also give in figure 4.5 the grouping produced by the system for adjective set 3 using the entire 21-million-word corpus but without any of the linguistic modules active. This partition is to be contrasted with the one given in figure 4.1 on page 73 which was produced from the same corpus and with the same number of clusters, but with all the linguistic modules active.

1. catastrophic harmful
2. dry wet
3. lenient rigid strict stringent
4. communist leftist
5. clever
6. abrupt chaotic disastrous gradual turbulent vigorous
7. affluent affordable inexpensive prosperous
8. outrageous
9. capitalist socialist
10. dismal gloomy pleasant
11. generous insufficient meager scant slim
12. delicate fragile

13. brilliant energetic
14. dual multiple stupid
15. hazardous toxic unreasonable unstable
16. plain
17. confusing
18. flexible hostile protracted unfriendly
19. endless
20. clean dirty impoverished
21. deadly fatal
22. astonishing misleading stunning
23. dumb fat smart
24. exotic

Figure 4.5
Partition with 24 clusters produced by the system for the adjective test set 3 of figure 4.4 using the entire 21-million-word corpus and no linguistic modules.

7 Cost of Incorporating the Linguistic Knowledge in the System

The cost of incorporating the linguistics-based modules in the system is not prohibitive. The effort needed to implement all the linguistic modules was about 5 person-months, in contrast with 7 person-months needed to develop the basic statistical system. Most of this time was spent in designing and implementing the finite-state grammar that is used for extracting adjective-noun and adjective-adjective pairs [Hatzivassiloglou, 1995b].

Furthermore, the run-time overhead caused by the linguistic modules is not significant. Each linguistic module takes from 1 to 7 minutes on a Sun SparcStation 10 to process a million items (words or pairs of words, as appropriate for the module), and all except the negative knowledge module need process a corpus only once, reusing the same information for different problem instances (word sets). This should be compared to the approximately 15 minutes needed by the statistical component for grouping about 40 adjectives.

8 Generalizing to Other Applications

In section 6 we showed that the introduction of linguistic knowledge in the word grouping system results in a performance difference that is not only statistically observable but also quantitatively significant (cf. table 4.4). We believe that these positive results should also apply to other corpus-based natural language processing systems that employ statistical methods.

Many statistical approaches share the same basic methodology with our system: a set of words is preselected, related words are identified in a corpus, the frequencies of words and of pairs of related words are estimated, and a statistical model is used to make predictions for the original words. Across applications, there are differences in what words are selected, how related words are defined, and what kinds of predictions are made. Nevertheless, the basic components stay the same. For example, in the adjective grouping application the original words are the adjectives and the predictions are their groups; in machine translation, the predictions are the translations of the words in the source language text; in sense disambiguation, the predictions are the senses assigned to the words of interest; in part-of-speech tagging or in classification, the predictions are the tags or classes assigned to each word. Because of this underlying similarity, the comparative analysis presented in this chapter is relevant to all these problems.

For a concrete example, consider the case of collocation extraction that has been addressed with statistical methods in the past. Smadja [1993] describes a system that initially uses the "nouns in vicinity" extraction model to collect co-occurrence information about words, and then identifies collocations on the basis of distributional criteria. A later component filters the retrieved collocations, removing the ones where the participating words are not used consistently in the same syntactic relationship. This post-processing stage doubles the precision of the system. We believe that using from the start a more sophisticated extraction model to collect these pairs of related words will have similar positive effects. Other linguistic components, such as a morphology module that combines frequency counts, should also improve the performance of that system. In this way, we can benefit from linguistic knowledge without having to use a separate filtering process after expending the effort to collect the collocations.

Similarly, the sense disambiguation problem is typically attacked by comparing the distribution of the neighbors of a word's occurrence to prototypical distributions associated with each of the word's senses [Gale et al., 1992b; Schütze, 1992]. Usually, no explicit linguistic knowledge is used in defining these neighbors, which are taken as all words appearing within a window of fixed width centered at the word being disambiguated.[10] Many words unrelated to the word of interest are collected in this way. In contrast, identifying appropriate word classes that can be expected on linguistic grounds to convey significant information about the original word should increase the performance of the disambiguation system. Such classes might be modified nouns for adjectives, nouns in a subject or object position for verbs, etc. As we have shown in section 6, less but more accurate information increases the quality of the results.

An interesting topic is the identification of parallels of the linguistic modules that have been designed with the present system in mind for these applications, at least for those modules which, unlike morphology, are not ubiquitous. Negative knowledge, for example, improves the performance of our system, supplementing the positive information provided by adjective-noun pairs. It could be useful for other systems as well if an appropriate application-dependent method of extracting such information is identified.

---

10. Although some researchers have used limited linguistic knowledge in selecting, processing, and classifying these neighbors; see, for example, [Hearst, 1991] and [Yarowsky, 1994].

9 Conclusions and Future Work

We have shown that all linguistic features considered in this study had a positive contribution to the performance of the system. Except for spell-checking, all these contributions were both statistically significant and large enough to make a difference in practical situations. The cost of incorporating the linguistics-based modules in the system is not prohibitive, both in terms of development time and in terms of actual run-time overhead. Furthermore, the results can be expected to generalize to a wide variety of corpus-based systems for different applications.

We should note here that in our comparative experiments we have focused on analyzing the benefits of symbolic knowledge that is readily available and can be efficiently incorporated into the system. We have avoided using lexical semantic knowledge because it is not generally available and because its use would defeat the very purpose of the word grouping system. However, on the basis of the measurable performance difference offered by the shallow linguistic knowledge we studied, it is reasonable to conjecture that deeper linguistic knowledge, if it becomes readily accessible, would probably increase the performance of a hybrid system even more.

In the future, we plan to extend the results discussed in this chapter with an analysis of the dependence of the effects of each parameter on the values of the other parameters. We are currently stratifying the experimental data obtained to study trends in the magnitude of parameter effects as other parameters vary in a controlled manner, and we will examine the interactions with corpus size and specificity of clustered adjectives. Preliminary results indicate that the importance of linguistic knowledge remains high even with large corpora, showing that we cannot offset the advantages of linguistic knowledge just by increasing the corpus size. We plan to investigate these trends and interactions with extended experiments in the future.

Acknowledgments

This work was supported jointly by the Advanced Research Projects Agency and the Office of Naval Research under grant N00014-89-J-1782, by the Office of Naval Research under grant N00014-95-1-0745, and by the National Science Foundation under grant GER-90-24069. It was performed under the auspices of the Columbia University CAT in High Performance Computing and Communications in Healthcare, a New York State Center for Advanced Technology

supported by the New York State Science and Technology Foundation. Any
opinions, findings, conclusions, or recommendations expressed in this publication are mine and do not necessarily reflect the views of the New York State
Science and Technology Foundation. I thank Kathy McKeown, Jacques
Robin, the anonymous reviewers, and the Balancing Act workshop organizers
and editors of this book for providing useful comments on earlier versions of
the chapter.

References

Roberto Basili, Maria Teresa Pazienza, and Paola Velardi. The Noisy Channel and the
Braying Donkey. In *Proceedings of the ACL Workshop The Balancing Act: Combining
Symbolic and Statistical Approaches to Language,* pp. 21–28, Las Cruces, New Mex-
ico, July 1994, Association for Computational Linguistics.

Peter F. Brown, Vincent J. della Pietra, Peter V. de Souza, Jennifer C. Lai, and Robert
L. Mercer. Class-Based *n*-gram Models of Natural Language. *Computational Linguistics,* 18(4): 467–479, 1992.

Kenneth W. Church. A Stochastic Parts Program and Noun Phrase Parser for Unrestricted Text. In *Proceedings of the Second Conference on Applied Natural Language
Processing,* pp. 136–143, Austin, Texas, February 1988.

Douglas R. Cutting, Julian M. Kupiec, Jan O. Pedersen, and Penelope Sibun. A Practical Part-of-Speech Tagger. In *Proceedings of the Third Conference on Applied Natural
Language Processing,* pp. 133–140, Trent, Italy, April 1992.

Norman R. Draper and Harry Smith. *Applied Regression Analysis,* 2nd edition, New
York, Wiley, 1981.

Michael Elhadad. Generating Adjectives to Express the Speaker's Argumentative
Intent. In *Proceedings of the 9th National Conference on Artificial Intelligence (AAAI-
91),* pp. 98–104, Anaheim, California, July 1991. American Association for Artificial
Intelligence.

William B. Frakes and Ricardo Baeza-Yates, editors. *Information Retrieval: Data
Structures and Algorithms.* Englewood Cliffs, N.J., Prentice Hall, 1992.

William A. Gale, Kenneth W. Church, and David Yarowsky. Estimating Upper and
Lower Bounds on the Performance of Word-Sense Disambiguation Programs. In *Pro-
ceedings of the 30th Annual Meeting of the ACL,* pp. 249–256, Newark, Del., June 1992.
Association for Computational Linguistics.

William A. Gale, Kenneth W. Church, and David Yarowsky. Work on Statistical Methods for Word Sense Disambiguation. In *Probabilistic Approaches to Natural Language: Papers from the 1992 Fall Symposium,* pp. 54–60, Cambridge, Massachusetts,
October 1992. Menlo Park, Calif., American Association for Artificial Intelligence,
AAAI Press, 1992.

Jean Dickinson Gibbons and Subhabrata Chakraborti. *Nonparametric Statistical Inference,* 3rd edition, New York, Marcel Dekker, 1992.

Vasileios Hatzivassiloglou. Automatic Retrieval of Semantic and Scalar Word Groups from Free Text. Technical Report CUCS-018-95, New York, Columbia University, 1995.

Vasileios Hatzivassiloglou. Retrieving Adjective-Noun, Adjective-Adjective, and Adjective-Adverb Syntagmatic Relationships from Corpora: Extraction via a Finite-State Grammar, Heuristic Selection, and Morphological Processing. Technical Report CUCS-019-95, New York, Columbia University, 1995.

Vasileios Hatzivassiloglou and Kathleen McKeown. Towards the Automatic Identification of Adjectival Scales: Clustering Adjectives According to Meaning. In *Proceedings of the 31st Annual Meeting of the ACL,* pp. 172–182, Columbus, Ohio, June 1993. Association for Computational Linguistics.

Marti A. Hearst. Noun Homograph Disambiguation Using Local Context in Large Text Corpora. In *Proceedings of the 7th Annual Conference of the University of Waterloo Centre for the the New OED and Text Research: Using Corpora,* Oxford, 1991.

Charles R. Hicks. *Fundamental Concepts in the Design of Experiments,* 3rd edition, New York, Holt, Rinehart, and Wilson, 1982.

Donald Hindle. Noun Classification from Predicate-Argument Structures. In *Proceedings of the 28th Annual Meeting of the ACL,* pp. 268–275, Pittsburgh, June 1990. Association for Computational Linguistics.

Julia B. Hirshberg. *A Theory of Scalar Implicature.* PhD thesis, Department of Computer and Information Science, University of Pennsylvania, Philadelphia, 1985.

Leonard Kaufman and Peter J. Rousseeuw. *Finding Groups in Data: An Introduction to Cluster Analysis.* New York, Wiley, 1990.

Maurice G. Kendall. A New Measure of Rank Correlation. *Biometrika,* 30: 81–93, 1938.

Maurice G. Kendall. *Rank Correlation Methods,* 4th edition. London, Griffin, 1975.

Kevin Knight and Steve K. Luk. Building a Large-Scale Knowledge Base for Machine Translation. In *Proceedings of the 12th National Conference on Artificial Intelligence (AAAI-94),* vol. 1, pp. 773–778, Seattle, July–August 1994. American Association for Artificial Intelligence.

Julian M. Kupiec. Robust Part-of-Speech Tagging Using a Hidden Markov Model. *Computer Speech and Language,* 6: 225–242, 1992.

Adrienne Lehrer. *Semantic Fields and Lexical Structure.* Amsterdam, North Holland, 1974.

Stephen C. Levinson. *Pragmatics.* Cambridge, England, Cambridge University Press, 1983.

Elizabeth D. Liddy and Woojin Paik. Statistically-Guided Word Sense Disambiguation. In *Probabilistic Approaches to Natural Language: Papers from the 1992 Fall Symposium,* pp. 98–107, Cambridge, Massachusetts, October 1992. Menlo Park, Calif., American Association for Artificial Intelligence, AAAI Press, 1992.

John Lyons. *Semantics,* vol. 1. Cambridge, England, Cambridge University Press, 1977.

Igor A. Mel'čuk and Nikolaj V. Pertsov. *Surface Syntax of English: a Formal Model within the Meaning-Text Framework.* Amsterdam, Benjamins, 1987.

George A. Miller, Richard Beckwith, Christiane Fellbaum, Derek Gross, and Katherine J. Miller. Introduction to WordNet: An On-Line Lexical Database. *International Journal of Lexicography (special issue),* 3(4): 235–312, 1990.

Johanna D. Moore. Personal communication. June 1993.

Rebecca J. Passonneau and Diane J. Litman. Intention-Based Segmentation: Human Reliability and Correlation with Linguistic Cues. In *Proceedings of the 31st Annual Meeting of the ACL,* pp. 148–155, Columbus, Ohio, June 1993. Association for Computational Linguistics.

Fernando Pereira, Naftali Tishby, and Lillian Lee. Distributional Clustering of English Words. In *Proceedings of the 31st Annual Meeting of the ACL,* pp. 183–190, Columbus, Ohio, June 1993. Association for Computational Linguistics.

Philip Resnik. Semantic Classes and Syntactic Ambiguity. In *Proceedings of the ARPA Workshop on Human Language Technology,* pp. 278–283, Plainsboro, N.J., March 1993. ARPA Software and Intelligent Systems Technology Office, San Francisco, Morgan Kaufmann, 1993.

Philip Resnik and Marti A. Hearst. Structural Ambiguity and Conceptual Relations. In *Proceedings of the ACL Workshop on Very Large Corpora,* pp. 58–64, Columbus, Ohio, June 1993. Association for Computational Linguistics.

Victor Sadler. *Working with Analogical Semantics: Disambiguation Techniques in DLT.* Dordrecht, The Netherlands, Foris Publications, 1989.

Hinrich Schütze. Word Sense Disambiguation With Sublexical Representations. In *Proceedings of the AAAI-92 Workshop on Statistically-Based NLP Techniques,* pp. 109–113, San Jose, Calif., July 1992. American Association for Artificial Intelligence.

John M. Sinclair (editor in chief). *Collins COBUILD English Language Dictionary.* London, Collins, 1987.

Frank Smadja. Retrieving Collocations from Text: Xtract. *Computational Linguistics,* 19(1): 143–177, March 1993.

Helmuth Späth. *Cluster Dissection and Analysis: Theory, FORTRAN Programs, Examples.* Chichester, West Sussex, England, Ellis Horwood, 1985.

Jost Trier. Das sprachliche Feld. Eine Auseinandersetzung. *Neue Jahrbücher für Wissenschaft und Jugendbildung,* 10: 428–449, 1934.

C. J. van Rijsbergen. *Information Retrieval,* 2nd edition, London, Butterworths, 1979.

Alex Waibel and Kai-Fu Lee, editors. *Readings in Speech Recognition.* San Mateo, Calif., Morgan Kaufmann, 1990.

David Yarowsky. Decision Lists for Lexical Ambiguity Resolution: Application to Accent Restoration in Spanish and French. In *Proceedings of the 32nd Annual Meeting of the ACL,* pp. 88–95, Las Cruces, N.M., June 1994. Association for Computational Linguistics.

Chapter 5

The Automatic Construction   Shyam Kapur and Robin Clark
of a Symbolic Parser
via Statistical Techniques

At the core of contemporary generative syntax is the premise that all languages obey a set of universal principles, and syntactic variation among languages is confined to a finite number of parameters. On this model, a child's acquisition of the syntax of his or her native language depends on identifying the correct parameter settings for that language based on observation—for example, determining whether to form questions by placing question words at the beginning of the sentence (e.g., English: Who did Mary say John saw) or leaving them syntactically in situ (e.g., Chinese: Mary said John saw who). Prevalent work on parameter setting focuses on the way that observed events in the child's input might "trigger" settings for parameters (e.g. [Manzini and Wexler, 1987]), to the exclusion of inductive or distributional analyses.

In "The Automatic Construction of a Symbolic Parser via Statistical Techniques," Kapur and Clark build on their previous work on proving learnability results in a stochastic setting [Kapur, 1991] and exploring the complexity of parameter setting in the face of realistic assumptions about how parameters interact [Clark, 1992]. Here they combine forces to present a learning model in which distributional evidence plays a critical role—while still adhering to an orthodox, symbolic view of language acquisition consistent with the Chomskian paradigm. Notably, they validate their approach by means of an implemented model, tested on naturally occurring data of the kind available to child language learners.—Eds.

1 Motivation

We report on the progress we have made toward developing a robust "self-constructing" parsing device that uses indirect negative evidence [Kapur and Bilardi, 1991] to set its *parameters*. Generally, by parameter we mean any point of variation between languages; that is, a property on which two languages may differ. Thus, the relative placement of an object with respect to the verb, a determiner with respect to a noun, the difference between prepositional and postpositional languages and the presence of long-distance anaphors like Japanese "zibun" and Icelandic "sig" are all parameters. A self-constructing parsing device would be exposed to an input text consisting of simple unpreprocessed sentences. On the basis of this text, the device would induce indirect negative evidence in support of some one parsing device located in the parameter space.

The development of a self-constructing parsing system would have a number of practical and theoretical benefits. First, such a parsing device would reduce the development costs of new parsers. At the moment, grammars must be developed by hand, a technique requiring a significant investment in money and man-hours. If a basic parser could be developed automatically, costs would be reduced significantly, even if the parser required some fine-tuning after the initial automatic learning procedure. Second, a parser capable of self-modification is potentially more robust when confronted with novel or semigrammatical input. This type of parser would have applications in information retrieval as well as language instruction and grammar correction. As far as linguistic theory is concerned, the development of a parser capable of self-modification would give us considerable insight into the formal properties of complex systems as well as the twin problems of language learnability and language acquisition, the research problems that have provided the foundation of generative grammar.

Given a linguistic parameter space, the problem of locating a target language somewhere in the space on the basis of a text consisting of only grammatical sentences is far from trivial. Clark [1990, 1992] has shown that the complexity of the problem is potentially exponential because the relationship between the points of variation and the actual data can be quite indirect and tangled. Since, given n parameters, there are 2^n possible parsing devices, enumerative search through the space is clearly impossible. Because each datum may be successfully parsed by a number of different parsing devices within the space and because the surface properties of grammatical strings underdetermine the properties of the parsing device which must be fixed by the learning algorithm, standard deductive machine learning techniques are as complex as a brute enumerative search [Clark, 1992, 1994a]. In order to solve this problem, robust techniques that can rapidly eliminate inferior hypotheses must be developed.

We propose a learning procedure that unites symbolic computation with statistical tools. Historically, symbolic techniques have proved to be a versatile tool in natural language processing. These techniques have the disadvantage of being both brittle (easily broken by new input or by user error) and costly (as grammars are extended to handle new constructions, development becomes more difficult owing to the complexity of rule interactions within the grammar). Statistical techniques have the advantage of robustness, although the resulting grammars may lack the intuitive clarity found in symbolic systems. We propose to fuse the symbolic and statistical techniques, a development we view both as inevitable and welcome; the resulting system will use statistical learning techniques to output a symbolic parsing device. We view this development to provide a nice middle ground between the problems of overtraining vs. undertraining. That is, statistical approaches to learning often tend to overfit the training set of data. Symbolic approaches, on the other hand, tend to behave as though they were undertrained (breaking down on novel input) since the grammar tends to be compact. Combining statistical techniques with symbolic parsing would give the advantage of obtaining relatively compact descriptions (symbolic processing) with robustness (statistical learning) that is not overtuned to the training set.

We believe that our approach not only provides a new technique of obtaining robust parsers in natural language systems but also provides partial explanation for child language acquisition. Traditionally, in either of these separate fields of inquiry, two widely different approaches have been pursued. One of them is largely statistical and heavily data-driven; another one is largely symbolic and theory-driven. Neither approach has proved exceptionally successful in either field. Our approach not only bridges the symbolic and statistical approaches but also tries to bring closer the two disparate fields of inquiry.

We claim that the final outcome of the learning process is a grammar that is not simply some predefined template with slots that have been filled in but rather crucially a product of the process itself. The result of setting a parameter to a certain value involves not just the fixing of that parameter but also a potential reorganization of the grammar to reflect the new parameter's values. The final result must not only be any parser consistent with the parameter values but one that is also self-modifiable and furthermore one that can modify itself along one of many directions depending on the subsequent input. Exactly for this reason, the relevance of our solution to a purely engineering solution to parser building remains—the parser builder cannot simply look up the parameter values in a table. In fact, parameter setting has to be a part, even just a small part, of the parser construction process. If this were not the case, we probably would have had little difficulty in building excellent parsers for individual languages. Equally, the notion of self-modification is of enormous interest to linguistic typologists and diachronic linguists. In particular, a careful study of self-modification would place substantive limits on linguistic variation and on the ways in which languages could, in principle, change over time. The information-theoretic analysis of linguistic variation is still in its infancy, but it promises to provide an important theoretical tool for linguists. (See [Clark and Roberts, in preparation] for applications to linguistic typology and diachronic change.)

As far as child language acquisition is concerned, viewing the parameter setting problem in an information-theoretic light seems to be the best perspective one can put together for this problem [Clark, 1994b; Kapur and Clark, in press]. Linguistic representations carry information, universal grammar encodes information about all natural languages, and the linguistic input from the target language must carry information about the target language in some form. The task of the learner can be viewed as that of efficiently and accurately decoding the information contained in the input in order to have enough information to build the grammar for the target language.

To date, the information-theoretic principles underlying the entire process have not received adequate attention. For example, the most commonly considered learning algorithm is one that simply moves from one parameter setting to another parameter setting based only on failure in parsing. That such an algorithm is entirely implausible empirically is one issue; in addition, it can be shown that one of the fastest ways for this algorithm to converge is to take a random walk in the parameter space, which is clearly grossly inefficient. Such an approach is also inconsistent with a maxim true about much of learning: "We learn at the edge of what we already know." Furthermore, in no sense would one be able to maintain that there is a monotonic increase in the information the child has about the target language in any real sense. We know from observation and experimentation that children's learning appears to be largely monotonic and fairly uniform across children. Finally and most important, these algorithms fail to account for how certain information is necessary for children's learning to proceed from stage n to stage $n + 1$. Just as some background information is necessary for children's learning to proceed from stage 0 (the *initial state*) to stage 1, there is good reason to believe that there must be some background + acquired information that must be crucial to take the child from stage n to stage $n + 1$. In the algorithms we consider, we provide arguments that the child can proceed from one stage to the next only because at the earlier stage the child has been able to acquire enough information to be able to build enough structure. This, in turn, is necessary to in fact efficiently extract further information from the input to learn further.

The restrictive learning algorithms that we consider here allow the process of information extraction from a plausible input text to be investigated in both complete formal and computational detail. We hope to show that our work is leading the way to establish precisely the information-theoretic details of the entire learning process, from what the initial state needs to be to what can be learned and how. For example, another aspect in which previous attempts have been deficient is in their varying degrees of assumptions about what information the child has access to when in the initial state. We feel that the most logical approach is to assume that the child has no access to any information unless it can be argued that without some information, learning would be impossible or at least infeasible.

Some psycholinguistic consequences of our proposal appear to be empirically valid. For example, it has been observed that in relatively free word order languages such as Russian, the child first stabilizes on some word order, although not the same word order across children. Another linguistic and psycholinguistic consequence of this proposal is that there is no need to stipulate markedness or initial preset values. Extensional relationships between languages and their purported consequences, such as the *Subset Principle,* are irrelevant. Furthermore, *triggers* need not be single utterances; statistical properties of the corpus may trigger parameter values.

2   Preliminaries

In this section, we first list some parameters that give some idea of the kinds of variations between languages that we hope our system is capable of handling. We then illustrate why parameter setting is difficult by standard methods. This provides some additional explanation for the failure so far in developing a truly universal parameterized parser.

2.1   Linguistic Parameters

Naturally, a necessary preliminary to our work is to specify a set of parameters that will serve as a testing ground for the learning algorithm. This set of parameters must be embedded in a parsing system so that the learning algorithm can be tested against data sets that approximate the kind of input that parsing devices are likely to encounter in real-world applications.

Our goal, then, will be to first develop a prototype. We do not require that the prototype accept any arbitrarily selected language or that the coverage of the prototype parser be complete in any given language. Instead, we will develop a prototype with coverage that extends to some basic structures that any language learning device must account for, plus some structures that have proved difficult for various learning theories. In particular, given an already existing parser, we will extend its coverage by parameterizing it, as described below.

Our initial set of parameters will include the following other points of variation:

1. Relative order of specifiers and heads: This parameter covers the placement of determiners relative to nouns, relative position of the subject, and the placement of certain VP-modifying adverbs.

2. Relative order of heads and complements: This parameter deals with the position of objects relative to the verb (VO or OV orders), placement of nominal and adjectival complements, as well as the choice between prepositions and postpositions.

3. Scrambling: Some languages allow (relatively) free word order. For example, German has rules for displacing definite NPs and clauses out of their canonical positions. Japanese allows relatively free ordering of NPs and postpositional phrases so long as the verbal complex remains clause final. Other languages allow even freer word orders. We will focus on German and Japanese scrambling, bearing in mind that the model should be extendible to other types of scrambling.

4. Relative placement of negative markers and verbs: Languages vary as to where they place negative markers, like English *not*. English places its negative marker after the first tensed auxiliary, thus forcing *do* insertion when there is no other auxiliary, whereas Italian places negation after the tensed verb. French uses discontinuous elements like *ne . . . pas* or *ne . . . plus,* which are wrapped around the tensed verb or occur as continuous elements in infinitivals. The proper treatment of negation will require several parameters, given the range of variation.

5. Root word order changes: In general, languages allow for certain word order changes in root clauses but not in embedded clauses. An example of a root word order change is subject-auxiliary inversion in English, which occurs in root questions (*Did John leave?* vs. **I wonder did John leave?*). Another example would be inversion of the subject clitic with the tensed verb in French (*Quelle pomme a-t-il mangée* ["Which apple did he eat?"]) and the process of subject postposition and PP preposition in English (*A man walked into the room* vs. *Into the room walked a man*).

6. Rightward dislocation: This includes extraposition structures in English (*That John is late amazes me.* vs. *It amazes me that John is late.*), presentational *there* structures (*A man was in the park.* vs. *There was a man in the park.*), and stylistic inversion in French (*Quelle piste Marie a-t-elle choisie?*

["What path has Marie chosen?"]). Each of these constructions presents unique problems so that the entire data set is best handled by a system of interacting parameters.

7. Wh-movement vs. wh-in situ: Languages vary in the way they encode *wh*-questions. English obligatorily places one and only one *wh*-phrase (e.g., *who* or *which picture*) in first position. In French the wh-phrase may remain in place (in situ) although it may also form *wh*-questions as in English. Polish allows *wh*-phrases to be stacked at the beginning of the question.

8. Exceptional case marking, structural case marking: These parameters have little obvious effect on word order, but involve the treatment of infinitival complements. Thus, exceptional case marking and structural case marking allow for the generation of the order $V_{[+tense]}$ NP $VP_{[-tense]}$, where "$V_{[+tense]}$" is a tensed verb and "$VP_{[-tense]}$" is a VP headed by a verb in the infinitive. Both parameters involve the semantic relations between the NP and the infinitival VP as well as the treatment of case marking. These relations are reflected in constituent structure rather than word order and thus pose an interesting problem for the learning algorithm.

9. Raising and control: In the case of raising verbs and control verbs, the learner must correctly categorize verbs that occur in the same syntactic frame into two distinct groups based on semantic relations as reflected in the distribution of elements (e.g., idiom chunks) around the verbs.

10. Long- and short-distance anaphora: Short-distance anaphors, like "himself" in English, must be related to a coreferential NP within a constrained local domain. Long-distance anaphors (Japanese "zibun", Korean "caki") must also be related to a coreferential NP, but this NP need not be contained within the same type of local domain as in the short-distance case.

The above sampling of parameters has the virtue of being both small (and therefore possible to implement relatively quickly) and posing interesting learnability problems which will appropriately test our learning algorithm. Although the above list can be described succinctly, the set of possible targets will be large and a simple enumerative search through the possible targets will not be efficient.

2.2   Complexities of Parameter Setting

Theories based on the principles and parameters (*P&P*) paradigm hypothesize that languages share a central core of universal properties and that language variation can be accounted for by appeal to a finite number of points of variation, the so-called parameters. The parameters themselves may take on only a finite number of possible values, prespecified by Universal Grammar (UG). A fully specified *P&P* theory would account for language acquisition by hypothesizing that the learner sets parameters to the appropriate values by monitoring the input stream for "triggering data"; triggers are sentences which cause the learner to set a particular parameter to a particular value. For example, the imperative in (1) is a trigger for the order "V(erb) O(bject)":

(1) Kiss grandma.

under the hypothesis that the learner analyzes *grandma* as the patient of kissing and is predisposed to treat patients as structural objects.

Notice that trigger-based parameter setting presupposes that for each parameter p and each value v the learner can identify the appropriate trigger in the input stream. This is the problem of *trigger detection*. That is, given a particular input item, the learner must be able to recognize whether or not it is a trigger and, if so, what parameter and value it is a trigger for. Similarly, the learner must be able to recognize that a particular input datum is *not* a trigger for a certain parameter even though it may share many properties with a trigger. In order to make the discussion more concrete, consider the following example:

(2) a. John$_i$ thinks that Mary likes him$_i$.
    b. *John thinks that Mary$_j$ likes her$_j$.

English allows pronouns to be coreferent with a c-commanding nominal just in case that nominal is not contained within the same local syntactic domain as the pronoun; this is a universal property of pronouns and would seem to present little problem to the learner.

Note, however, that some languages, including Chinese, Icelandic, Japanese, and Korean, allow for long-distance anaphors. These are elements which are obligatorily coreferent with another nominal in the sentence, but which may be separated from that nominal by several clause boundaries. Thus, the following example from Icelandic is grammatical even though the anaphor *sig* is separated from its antecedent *Jón* by a clause boundary [Anderson, 1986]:

(3) Jón$_i$ segir ad María elski sig$_i$/hann$_i$
    John says that Mary loves self/him
    John says that Mary loves him.

Thus, UG includes a parameter that allows some languages to have long-distance anaphors and that, perhaps, fixes certain other properties of this class of anaphora.

Note that the example in (3) is of the same structure as the pronominal example in (2a). A learner whose target is English must not take examples like (2a) as a trigger for the long-distance anaphor parameter; what prevents the learner from being deceived? Why doesn't the learner conclude that English *him* is comparable to Icelandic *sig*? We would argue that the learner is sensitive to distributional evidence. For example, the learner is aware of examples like (4):

(4) John$_i$ likes him$_j$.

where the pronoun is not coreferential with anything else in the sentence. The existence of (4) implies that *him* cannot be a pure anaphor, long-distance or otherwise. Once the learner is aware of this distributional property of *him,* he or she can correctly rule out (2a) as a potential trigger for the long-distance anaphor parameter.

Distributional evidence, then, is crucial for parameter setting; no theory of parameter setting can avoid statistical properties of the input text. How far can we push the statistical component of parameter setting? In this chapter, we suggest that statistically based algorithms can be exploited to set parameters involving phenomena as diverse as word order, particularly verb second constructions, and cliticization, the difference between free pronouns and proclitics. The work reported here can be viewed as providing the basis for a theory of trigger detection; it seeks to establish a theory of the connection between the raw input text and the process of parameter setting.

3   Parameter-Setting Proposal

Let us suppose that there are n binary parameters each of which can take one of two values ('$+$' or '$-$') in a particular natural language. The core of a natural language is uniquely defined once all the n parameters have been assigned a value.[1]

Consider a random division of the parameters into some m groups. Let us call these groups $P_1, P_2, \ldots, P_m$. The Parameter-Setting Machine (PSM) first goes about setting all the parameters within the first group P_1 concurrently, as

---

1. Parameters can be looked at as fixed points of variation among languages. From a computational point of view, two different values of a parameter may simply correspond to two different bits of code in the parser. We are not committed to any particular scheme for the translation from a tuple of parameter values to the corresponding language. However, the sorts of parameters we consider have been listed in the previous section.

sketched below. After these parameters have been fixed, the machine next tries to set the parameters in group P_2 in similar fashion, and so on.

1. All parameters are unset initially, that is, there are no preset values. The parser is organized to only obey all the universal principles. At this stage, utterances from any possible natural language are accommodated with equal ease, but no sophisticated structure can be built.
2. Both the values of each of the parameters $p_i \in P_1$ are "competing" to establish themselves.
3. Corresponding to p_i, a pair of hypotheses are generated, say H^i_+ and H^i_-.
4. Next, these hypotheses are tested on the basis of input evidence.
5. If H^i_- fails or H^i_+ succeeds, set p_i's value to '+'. Otherwise, set p_i's value to '−'.

3.1   Formal Analysis of the PSM

We next consider a particular instantiation of the hypotheses and their testing. The way we have in mind involves constructing suitable window sizes during which the algorithm is sensitive to occurrence as well as non-occurrence of specific phenomena. Regular failure of a particular phenomenon to occur in a suitable window is one natural, robust kind of indirect negative evidence.

For example, the pair of hypotheses may be:

1. Hypothesis H^i_+: Expect not to observe phenomena from a fixed set O^i_- of phenomena which support the parameter value '−'.
2. Hypothesis H^i_-: Expect not to observe phenomena from a fixed set O^i_+ of phenomena which support the parameter value '+'.

Let w_i and k_i be two small numbers. Testing the hypothesis H^i_+ involves the following procedure:

1. A window of size w_i sentences is constructed and a record is maintained whether or not a phenomenon from within the set O^i_- occurred among those w_i sentences.
2. This construction of the window is repeated k_i different times and a tally c_i is made of the fraction of times the phenomena occurred at least once in the duration of the window.
3. The hypothesis H_+ succeeds if and only if the ratio of c_i to k_i is less than 0.5.

Note that the phenomena under scrutiny are assumed to be such that the parser is always capable of analyzing (to whatever extent necessary) the input. This is because in our view the parser consists of a fixed, core program whose behavior can be modified by selecting from among a finite set of "flags" (the parameters). Therefore, even if not all of the flags have been set to the correct values, the parser is such that it can at least partially represent the input. Thus, the parser is always capable of analyzing the input. Also, there is no need to explicitly store any input evidence. Suitable window sizes can be constructed during which the algorithm is sensitive to occurrence as well as non-occurrence of specific phenomena. By using windows, just the relevant bit of information from the input is extracted and maintained. (For detailed argumentation that this is a reasonable theoretical argument, see [Kapur and Bilardi, 1991; Kapur, 1993].) Note also that we have only sketched and analyzed a particular, simple version of our algorithm. In general, a whole range of window sizes may be used and this may be governed by the degree to which the different hypotheses have earned corroboration. (For some ideas along this direction in a more general setting, see [Kapur, 1991; Kapur and Bilardi, 1992].)

3.2   Order in Which Parameters Get Set
Note that in our approach certain parameters get set quicker than others. These are the ones that are expressed very frequently. It is possible that these parameters also make the information extraction more efficient quicker, for example, by enabling structure building so that other parameters can be set. If our proposal is right, then, for example, the word-order parameters which are presumably the very first ones to be set must be set based on a very primitive parser capable of handling any natural language. At this early stage, it may be that word and utterance boundaries cannot be reliably recognized and the lexicon is quite rudimentary. Furthermore, the only accessible property in the input stream may be the linear word order. Another particular difficulty with setting word-order parameters is that the surface order of constituents in the input does not necessarily reflect the underlying word order. For example, even though Dutch and German are SOV languages, there is a preponderance of SVO forms in the input due to the V2 (verb-second) phenomenon. The finite verb in root clauses moves to the second position and then the first position can be occupied by the subject, objects (direct or indirect), adverbials, or prepositional phrases. As we shall see, it is important to note that if the subject is not in the first position in a V2 language, it is most likely in the first position to the right of the verb. Finally, it has been shown by Gibson and Wexler [1992] that the parameter space created by the head-direction parameters along with the V2 parameter has *local maxima,* that is, incorrect parameter settings from which the learner can never escape.

3.3 Computational Analysis of the PSM

3.3.1 V2 Parameter

In this section, we summarize results we have obtained which show that word-order parameters can plausibly be set in our model.[2] The key concept we use is that of *entropy,* an information-theoretic statistical measure of randomness of a random variable. The entropy $H(X)$ of a random variable X, measured in bits, is $-\sum_X p(x) \log p(x)$. To give a concrete example, the outcome of a fair coin has an entropy of $-(.5 * \log(.5) + .5 * \log(.5)) = 1$ bit. If the coin is not fair and has .9 chance of heads and .1 chance of tails, then the entropy is around .5 bit. There is less uncertainty with the unfair coin—it is most likely going to turn up heads. Entropy can also be thought of as the number of bits on the average required to describe a random variable. Entropy of one variable, say X, conditioned on another, say Y, denoted as $H(X \mid Y)$, is a measure of how much better the first variable can be predicted when the value of the other variable is known.

We considered the possibility that by investigating the behavior of the entropy of positions in the neighborhood of verbs in a language, word-order characteristics of that language may be discovered.[3] For a V2 language, we expect that there will be more entropy to the left of the verb than to its right, that is, the position to the left will be less predictable than the one to the right. We first show that using a simple distributional analysis technique based on the five verbs the algorithm is assumed to know, another 15 words, most of which turn out to be verbs, can readily be obtained.

Consider the input text as generating tuples of the form (v, d, w), where v is one of the top 20 words (most of which are verbs), d is either the position to the left of the verb or to the right, and w is the word at that position.[4] V, D, and W are the corresponding random variables.

---

2. Preliminary results obtained with Eric Brill were presented at the 1993 Georgetown Roundtable on Language and Linguistics: Pre-session on Corpus-based Linguistics.

3. In the competition model for language acquisition [MacWhinney, 1987], the child considers cues to determine properties of the language, but while these cues are reinforced in a statistical sense the cues themselves are not information-theoretic in the way that ours are. In some recent discussion of triggering, Niyogi and Berwick [1993] formalize parameter setting as a Markov process. Crucially, there again the statistical assumption on the input is merely used to ensure that convergence is likely and triggers are simple sentences.

4. We thank Steve Abney for suggesting this formulation to us.

The procedure for setting the V2 parameter is the following:

If $H(W \mid V, D = left) > H(W \mid V, D = right)$ **then** $+$ V2 **else** $-$V2.

On each of the nine languages on which it has been possible to test our algorithm, the correct result was obtained. (Only the last three languages in table 5.1 are V2 languages.) Furthermore, in almost all cases, paired t-tests showed that the results were statistically significant. The amount (only 3000 utterances) and the quality of the input (unstructured unannotated input caretaker speech subcorpus from the CHILDES database [MacWhinney, 1991]), and the computational resources needed for parameter setting to succeed are psychologically plausible. Further tests were successfully conducted in order to establish both the robustness and the simplicity of this learning algorithm. It is also clear that once the value of the V2 parameter has been correctly set, the input is far more revealing with regard to other word-order parameters and they too can be set using similar techniques.

In order to make clear how this procedure fits into our general parameter-setting proposal, we spell out what the hypotheses are. In the case of the V2 parameter, the two hypotheses are not separately necessary since one hypothesis is the exact complement of the other. So the hypothesis H_+ may be as shown.

Hypothesis H_+: Expect not to observe that the entropy to the left of the verbs is lower than that to the right.

The window size that may be used could be around 300 utterances and the number of repetitions need to be around 10. Our previous results provide empirical support that this should suffice.

Table 5.1
The conditional entropy results

	$H(W \mid V, D =$ left)	$H(W \mid V, D =$ right)
English	4.22	4.26
French	3.91	5.09
Italian	4.91	5.33
Polish	4.09	5.78
Tamil	4.01	5.04
Turkish	3.69	4.91
Dutch	4.84	3.61
Danish	4.42	4.24
German	5.55	4.97

By assuming that besides knowing a few verbs, as before, the algorithm also recognizes some of the first and second person pronouns of the language, we cannot only determine aspects of the pronoun system (see section 3.3.2) but also get information about the V2 parameter. The first step of learning is the same as above; that is, the learner acquires additional verbs based on distributional analysis. We expect that in the V2 languages (Dutch and German), the pronouns will appear more often immediately to the right of the verb than to the left. For French, English, and Italian, exactly the reverse is predicted. Our results (2-1 or better ratio in the predicted direction) confirm these predictions.[5]

3.3.2 Clitic Pronouns We now show that our techniques can lead to straightforward identification and classification of clitic pronouns.[6] In order to correctly set the parameters governing the syntax of pronominals, the learner must distinguish clitic pronouns from free and weak pronouns as well as sort all pronoun systems according to their proper case system (e.g., nominative pronouns, accusative pronouns). Furthermore, the learner must have some reliable method for identifying the presence of clitic pronouns in the input stream. The algorithm we report, which is also based on the observation of entropies of positions in the neighborhood of pronouns, not only distinguishes accurately between clitic and freestanding pronouns but also successfully sorts clitic pronouns into linguistically natural classes.

It is assumed that the learner knows a set of first and second person pronouns. The learning algorithm computes the entropy profile for three positions to the left and right of the pronouns ($H(W \mid P = p)$ for the six different positions, where p's are the individual pronouns. These profiles are then compared and those pronouns that have similar profiles are clustered together. Interestingly, it turns out that the clusters are syntactically appropriate categories.

In French, for example, based on the Pearson correlation coefficients we could deduce that the object clitics *me* and *te,* the subject clitics *je* and *tu,* the non-clitics *moi* and *toi,* and the ambiguous pronouns *nous* and *vous* are most closely related only to the other element in their own class.

---

5. We also verified that the object clitics in French were not primarily responsible for the correct result.

6. Preliminary results were presented at the Berne workshop on L1- and L2-acquisition of clause-internal rules: scrambling and cliticization in January 1994.

	VOUS	TOI	MOI	ME	JE	TU	TE	NOUS
VOUS	1							
TOI	0.62	1						
MOI	0.57	0.98	1					
ME	0.86	0.24	0.17	1				
JE	0.28	0.89	0.88	-0.02	1			
TU	0.41	0.94	0.94	0.09	0.97	1		
TE	0.88	0.39	0.30	0.95	0.16	0.24	1	
NOUS	0.91	0.73	0.68	0.82	0.53	0.64	0.87	1

In fact, the entropy signature for the ambiguous pronouns can be analyzed as a mathematical combination of the signatures for the conflated forms. To distinguish clitics from non-clitics we use the measure of *stickiness* (proportion of times they are sticking to the verbs compared to the times they are two or three positions away). These results are quite good. The stickiness is as high as 54% to 55% for the subject clitics; non-clitics have stickiness no more than 17%.

The results can be seen most dramatically if we chart the conditional entropy of positions around the pronoun in question. Figure 5.1 shows the unambiguous freestanding pronouns *moi* and *toi*.

Compare *moi*, the freestanding pronoun, the other first person pronoun *je* (the nominative clitic), and *me* (the non-nominative clitic). The freestanding pronoun, *moi* is systematically less informative about its surrounding environment, corresponding to a slightly flatter curve than either *je* or *me*.

This distinction in the slopes of the curves is also apparent if we compare the curve associate with *toi* against the curves associated with *tu* (nominative) and *te* (non-nominative) in Figure 5.2; *toi* has the gentlest curve. This suggests that the learner could distinguish clitic pronouns from freestanding pronouns by checking for sharp drops in conditional entropy around the pronoun; clitics should stand out as having relatively sharp curves.

Note that we have three distinct curves in figure 5.3. We have already discussed the difference between clitic and freestanding pronouns. Do nominative and non-nominative clitics sort out by our method? Figure 5.3 suggests they might since *je* has a sharp dip in conditional entropy to its right, whereas *me* has a sharp dip to its left. Consider figure 5.4 where the conditional entropy of positions around *je, tu,* and *on* have been plotted. We have

UNAMBIGUOUS FREE-STANDING PRONOUNS

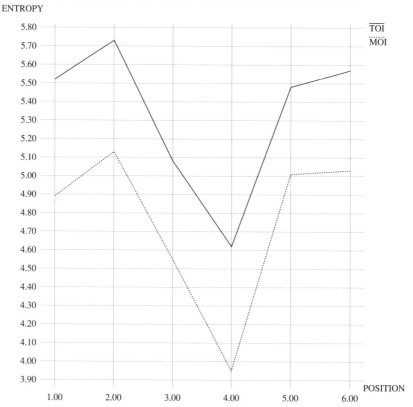

Figure 5.1
Entropy conditioned on position.

included *on* with the first and second person clitics since it is often used as a first person plural pronoun in colloquial French. All three are unambiguously nominative clitic pronouns. Note that their curves are basically identical, showing a sharp dip in conditional entropy one position to the right of the clitic.

Figure 5.5 shows the non-nominative clitic pronouns *me* and *te*. Once again, the curves are essentially identical, with a dip in entropy one position to the left of the clitic. The position to the left of the clitic will tend to be part of the subject (often a clitic pronoun in the sample we considered). Nevertheless, it is

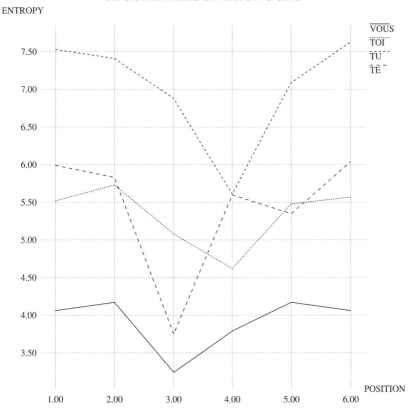

Figure 5.2
Entropy conditioned on position.

clear that the learner will have evidence to partition the clitic pronouns on the basis of where the dip in entropy occurs.

Let us turn, finally, to the interesting cases of *nous* and *vous*. These pronouns are unusual in that they are ambiguous between freestanding and clitic pronouns and, furthermore, may occur as either nominative or non-nominative clitics. We would expect them, therefore, to distinguish themselves from the other pronouns. If we consider the curve associated with *vous* in figure 5.2, it is immediately apparent that it has a fairly gentle slope, as one would expect of a freestanding pronoun. Nevertheless, the conditional entropy of

FIRST PERSON PRONOUNS

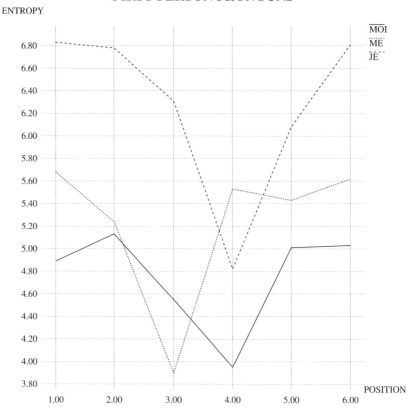

Figure 5.3
Entropy conditioned on position.

vous is rather low both to its right and its left, a property we associate with clitics; in fact, its conditional entropy is systematically lower than the unambiguous clitics *tu* and *te,* although this fact may be due to our sample. Figure 5.6 compares the conditional entropy of positions surrounding *vous* and *nous*. Once again, we see that *nous* and *vous* are associated with very similar curves.

Summarizing, we have seen that conditional entropy can be used to distinguish freestanding and clitic pronouns. This solves at least part of the learner's problem in that the method can form the basis for a practical algorithm for

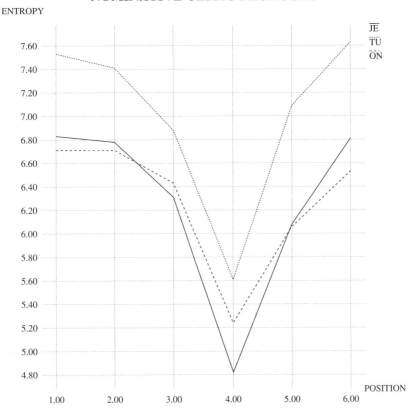

Figure 5.4
Entropy conditioned on position.

detecting the presence of clitics in the input stream. Furthermore, we have seen that conditional entropy can be used to break pronouns into further classes like nominative and non-nominative. The learner can use these calculations as a robust, noise-resistant means of setting parameters. Thus, at least part of the problem of trigger detection has been answered. The input is such that the learner can detect certain systematic cues and exploit them in determining grammatical properties of the target. At the very least, the learner could use these cues to form a "rough sketch" of the target grammar, allowing the learner to bootstrap its way to a full fledged grammatical system.

NON-NOMINATIVE CLITIC PRONOUNS

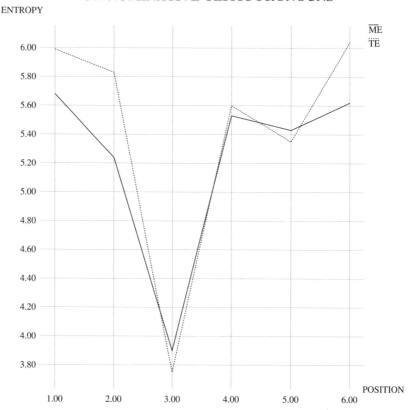

Figure 5.5
Entropy conditioned on position.

The Dutch clitic system is far more complicated than the French pronoun system (see, e.g., [Zwart, 1993]). Even so, our entropy calculations made some headway toward classifying the pronouns. We are able to distinguish the weak and strong subject pronouns. Since even the strong subject pronouns in Dutch tend to stick to their verbs very closely and two clitics can come next to each other, the raw stickiness measure seems to be inappropriate. Although the Dutch case is problematic owing to the effects of V2 and scrambling, we are in the process of treating these phenomena and anticipate that the pronoun calculations in Dutch will sort out properly once the influence of these other word-order processes are factored in appropriately.

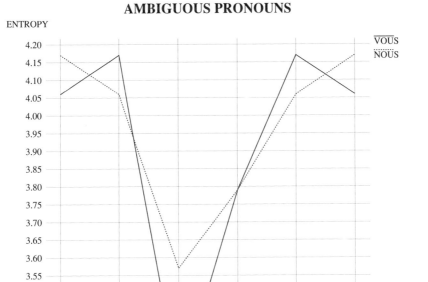

Figure 5.6
Entropy conditioned on position.

4   Conclusions

It needs to be emphasized that in our statistical procedure there is a mechanism available to the learning mechanism by which it can determine when it has seen enough input to reliably determine the value of a certain parameter. (Such means are nonexistent in any trigger-based error-driven learning theory.) In principle at least, the learning mechanism can determine the variance in the quantity of interest as a function of the text size and then know when enough text has been seen to be sure that a certain parameter has to be set in a particular way.

We are currently extending the results we have obtained to other parameters and other languages. We are convinced that the word-order parameters [e.g., (1) and (2)] should be fairly easy to set and amenable to an information-theoretic analysis along the lines sketched earlier. Scrambling also provides a case where calculations of entropy should provide an immediate solution to the parameter-setting problem. Note however that both scrambling and V2 interact in an interesting way with the basic word-order parameters; a learner may be potentially misled by both scrambling and V2 into missetting the basic word order parameters since both parameters can alter the relationship between heads, their complements, and their specifiers.

Parameters involving adverb placement, extraposition, and wh-movement should be relatively more challenging to the learning algorithm given the relatively low frequency with which adverbs are found in adult speech to children. These cases provide good examples which motivate the use of multiple trials by the learner. The interaction between adverb placement and head movement, then, will pose an interesting problem for the learner since the two parameters are interdependent; what the learner assumes about adverb placement is contingent on what it assumes about head placement and vice versa.

Acknowledgments

We firstly thank two anonymous referees for some very useful comments. We are also indebted to Isabella Barbier, Eric Brill, Bob Frank, Aravind Joshi, Barbara Lust, and Philip Resnik along with the audience at the Balancing Act workshop at the Annual meeting of the Association of Computational Linguistics for comments on various parts of this chapter.

References

Anderson, S. 1986. The typology of anaphoric dependencies: Icelandic (and other) reflexives. In L. Hellan and K. Christensen, editors. *Topics in Scandinavian Syntax,* pp. 65–88. Dordrecht, The Netherlands, D. Reidel.

Robin Clark. 1990. Papers on learnability and natural selection. *Technical Report 1,* Université de Genève, Département de Linguistique générale et de linguistique française, Faculté des Lettres, CH-1211, Genève 4, 1990. Technical Reports in Formal and Computational Linguistics.

Robin Clark. 1992. The selection of syntactic knowledge. *Language Acquisition,* 2(2): 83–149.

Robin Clark. 1994a. Hypothesis formation as adaptation to an environment: Learnability and natural selection. In Barbara Lust, Magui Suñer, and Gabriella Hermon, editors, *Syntactic Theory and First Language Acquisition: Crosslinguistic Perspectives.* Presented at the 1992 symposium on Syntactic Theory and First Language Acquisition: Cross Linguistic Perspectives at Cornell University, Ithaca. Hillsdale, N.J., Erlbaum.

Robin Clark. 1994b. Kolmogorov complexity and the information content of parameters. Technical Report. Philadelphia, Institute for Research in Cognitive Science, University of Pennsylvania, 1994.

Robin Clark and Ian Roberts. In preparation. *Complexity is the Engine of Variation,* manuscript. University of Pennsylvania, Philadelphia, and University of Wales, Bangor.

Edward Gibson and Kenneth Wexler. 1992. Triggers. Presented at GLOW. Linguistic Inquiry, 25, pp. 407–454.

Shyam Kapur. 1991. *Computational Learning of Languages.* Ph.D. thesis, Cornell University. Computer Science Department Technical Report 91-1234.

Shyam Kapur. 1993. How much of what? Is this what underlies parameter setting? In *Proceedings of the 25th Stanford University Child Language Research Forum.*

Shyam Kapur. 1994. Some applications of formal learning theory results to natural language acquisition. In Barbara Lust, Magui Suñer, and Gabriella Hermon, editors, *Syntactic Theory and First Language Acquisition: Crosslinguistic Perspectives.* Lawrence. Presented at the 1992 symposium on Syntactic Theory and First Language Acquisition: Cross Linguistic Perspectives at Cornell University. Hillsdale, N.J., Erlbaum.

Shyam Kapur and Gianfranco Bilardi. 1992. Language learning from stochastic input. In *Proceedings of the Fifth Conference on Computational Learning Theory.* San Mateo, Calif., Morgan-Kaufman.

Shyam Kapur and Robin Clark. In press. The Automatic Identification and Classification of Clitic Pronouns. Presented at the *Berne workshop on the L1- and L2-Acquisition of Clause-Internal Rules: Scrambling and Cliticization,* January 1994.

R. Manzini and K. Wexler. Parameters, binding theory, and learnability. *Linguistic Inquiry,* 18: 413–444, 1987.

Brian MacWhinney. 1987. The competition model. In Brian MacWhinney, editor, *Mechanisms of Language Acquisition.* Hillsdale, N.J., Erlbaum.

Brian MacWhinney. 1991. *The CHILDES Project: Tools for Analyzing Talk.* Hillsdale, N.J., Erlbaum.

Partha Niyogi and Robert C. Berwick. 1993. Formalizing triggers: A learning model for finite spaces. Technical Report A.I. Memo No. 1449. Cambridge, Mass., Institute of Technology. Also Center for Biological Computational Learning, Whitaker College Paper No. 86.

C. Jan-Wouter Zwart. 1993. Notes on clitics in Dutch. In Lars Hellan, editor, *Clitics in Germanic and Slavic,* pp. 119–155. Eurotyp Working Papers, Theme Group 8, vol. 4, University of Tilburg, The Netherlands.

Chapter 6

Combining Linguistic
with Statistical Methods
in Automatic Speech
Understanding

Patti Price

Speech understanding is an application that consists of two major components: the natural language processing component, which has traditionally been based on algebraic or symbolic approaches, and the speech recognition component, which has traditionally used statistical approaches. Price reviews the culture clash that has resulted as these two areas have been linked into the larger speech understanding task. Her position is that balancing the symbolic and the statistical will yield results that neither community could achieve alone.

Price points out that the best performing speech recognition systems have been based on statistical pattern matching techniques. At the same time, the most fully developed natural language analysis systems of the 1970s and 1980s were rule-based, using symbolic logic, and often requiring large sets of hand-crafted rules. When these two were put together in the late 1980s—most notably in the United States, in the context of projects funded by the Defense Advanced Research Projects Agency (DARPA)—the result was to have an effect on both communities. Initially, that effect tended to be the fostering of skepticism, as shown in Price's table 6.1, but increasingly the result has been a tendency to combine symbolic with statistical and engineering approaches. Price concludes her thoughtful review by presenting some of the challenges in achieving the balance and some of the compromises required by both the speech and natural language processing communities in order to reach their shared goal.—Eds.

1 Introduction: The Cultural Gap

This chapter presents an overview of automatic speech understanding techniques that combine symbolic approaches with statistical pattern matching methods. The two major component technologies in speech understanding arise from different cultural heritages: natural language (NL) understanding technology has traditionally used algebraic or symbolic approaches, and speech recognition technology has traditionally used statistical approaches. Integration of these technologies in speech understanding requires a "balancing act" that addresses cultural and technical differences among the component technologies and their representatives.

As argued in Price and Ostendorf [1995], representatives of symbolic approaches and of approaches based on statistical pattern matching may view each other with some suspicion. Psychologists and linguists, representing symbolic approaches, may view automatic algorithms as "uninteresting collections of ad hoc ungeneralizable methods for limited domains." The automatic speech recognition community, on the other hand, may argue that automatic speech recognition should not be modeled after human speech recognition; since the tasks and goals of machines are very different from those of humans, the methods should also be different. Thus, in this view, symbolic approaches are "uninteresting collections of ad hoc ungeneralizable methods for limited domains." The same words may be used, but mean different things, as indicated in table 6.1.

It is the thesis of this chapter that balancing the symbolic and the statistical approaches can yield results that neither community alone could achieve because:

• Statistical approaches alone may tend to ignore the important fact that spoken language is a social mechanism evolved for communication among entities whose biological properties constrain the possibilities. Mechanisms that are successful for machines are likely to share many properties with those successful for people, and much of our knowledge of human properties is expressed in symbolic form.
• Symbolic techniques alone may not be powerful enough to model complex human behavior; statistical approaches have many valuable traits to be leveraged.

Table 6.1
Cross-cultural mini-lexicon

	Linguists	Engineers
Uninteresting	Provides no explanation of cognitive processes.	Provides no useful applications.
Ad hoc	Without theoretical motivation.	Must be provided by hand.
Ungeneralizable	"Techniques that help you climb a tree may not help you get to the moon."	Expense of knowledge engineering prohibits assessing new or more complex domains.

After a brief historical survey (section 2), this chapter surveys the fields of speech recognition (section 3), of NL understanding (section 4), and of their integration (section 5), and concludes with a discussion of current challenges (section 6).

2 Historical Considerations

Activity and results in automatic speech understanding have increased in recent years. The DARPA (Defense Advanced Research Projects Agency) program merger of two previously independent programs (speech and NL) has had a profound impact. Previously, the speech recognition program focused on the automatic transcription of speech, whereas the NL understanding program focused on interpreting the meanings of typed input.

In the DARPA speech understanding program of the 1970s (see, e.g. [Klatt, 1977]), artificial intelligence (AI) was a relatively new field full of promise. Systems were developed by separating knowledge sources along traditional linguistic divisions: for example, acoustic phonetics, phonology, morphology, lexical access, syntax, semantics, discourse. The approach was largely symbolic and algebraic; rules were devised, measurements were made, thresholds were set, and decisions resulted. A key weakness of the approach proved to be the number of modules and the decision-making process. When each module is forced to make irrevocable decisions without interaction with other modules, errors can only propagate; a seven-stage serial process in which each module is 90% accurate has an overall accuracy of less than 50%. As statistical pattern matching techniques were developed and performed significantly better than the symbolic approaches with significantly less research investment, the funding focus and the research community's activities shifted.

The differences in performance between the two approaches during the 1970s could be viewed as a lesson for both symbolic and statistical approaches: making irrevocable decisions early (before considering more knowledge sources) can severely degrade performance. Statistical models provide a convenient mechanism for such delayed decision-making, and subsequent hardware and algorithmic developments enabled the consideration of increasingly larger sets of hypotheses. Although statistical models are certainly not the only tool for investigating speech and language, they do provide several important features:

• They can be trained automatically (provided there are data), which facilitates porting to new domains and uses.
• They can provide a systematic and convenient mechanism for combining multiple knowledge sources.

• They can express the more continuous properties of speech and language (e.g., prosody, vowel changes, and other sociolinguistic processes).
• They facilitate use of large corpora, which is important since the more abstract linguistic units are relatively rare compared to the phones modeled in speech recognition; hence large corpora are needed to provide enough instances to be modeled.
• They provide a means for assessing incomplete knowledge.
• They can provide a means for acquiring knowledge about speech and language.

The advantages summarized above are further elaborated in Price and Ostendorf [1995]. The biggest disadvantage of statistical models may be lack of familiarity to those more comfortable with symbolic approaches. The following sections outline how cultural and technical challenges are being met through a variety of approaches to speech, NL understanding, and their integration.

3   Speech Recognition Overview

For several years, the best performing speech recognition systems have been based on statistical pattern matching techniques [Pallett et al., 1990; Pallett, 1991; Pallett et al., 1992, 1993, 1994, 1995]. The most commonly used method is probably hidden Markov models (HMMs) (see, e.g. [Bahl et al., 1983; Rabiner 1989; Picone 1990]), although there is significant work using other pattern matching techniques (see, e.g. [Ostendorf and Roukos 1989; Zue et al., 1992]), including neural network–based approaches (see e.g. [Hampshire and Weibel 1990]) and hybrid HMM–neural network approaches (see e.g. [Abrash et al., 1994]). One can think of the symbolic components as representing our knowledge, and of the statistical components as representing our ignorance. The words, phones, and states chosen for the model are manipulated symbolically. Statistical methods are used to estimate automatically those aspects we cannot or do not want to model explicitly. Typically, development of recognition systems involves several issues. Samples are outlined below.

Feature Selection and Extraction   If the raw speech waveform is simply sampled in time and amplitude, there are far too much data; some feature extraction is needed. The most common features extracted are cepstral coefficients (derived from a spectral analysis), and derivatives of these coefficients. Although there has been some incorporation of knowledge of the human auditory system into feature extraction work, little has been done since the 1970s in implementing linguistically motivated features (e.g., high, low, front, back) in a recognition system. (See, however, the work of Ken Stevens and colleagues for significant work in this area not yet incorporated in automatic speech recognition systems [Stevens et al., 1992]). A representation of phones in terms of a small set of features has several advantages in speech recognition: fewer parameters could be better estimated given a fixed corpus; phones that are rare or unseen in the corpus could be estimated on the basis of the more frequently occurring features that compose them; and since features tend to change more slowly than phones, it is possible that sampling in time could be less frequent.

Acoustic and Phonetic Modeling A Markov model represents the probabilities of sequences of units, for example, words or sounds. The "hidden" Markov model, in addition, models the uncertainty of the current "state." By analogy with speech production, and using phones as states, the mechanism can be thought of as modeling two probabilities associated with each phone: the probability of the acoustics given the phone (to model the variability in the realization of phones), and the probability of transition to another phone given the current phone. Though some HMMs are used this way, most systems use states that are smaller than a phone (e.g., first, middle, and last part of a phone). Such models have more parameters, and hence can provide greater detail. Adding skips and loops to the states can model the temporal variability of the realization of phones. Given the model, parameters are estimated automatically from a corpus of data. Thus, models can be "tuned" to a particular (representative) sample, an important attribute for porting to new domains.

Model Inventory Although many systems model phones, or phones conditioned on the surrounding phonetic context, others claim improved performance through the selection of units or combination of units determined automatically or semiautomatically (see, e.g. [Bahl et al., 1991]). The SRI system combines phone models based on a hierarchy of linguistic contexts differing in detail, combined as a function of the amount of training data for each (see [Butzberger et al., 1992]).

Distributions In the HMM formulation, the state output distributions have been a topic of research interest. Generally speaking, modeling more detail improves performance, but requires more parameters to estimate, which in turn requires more data for robust estimation. Methods have been developed to reduce the number of parameters to estimate without degrading accuracy, some of which include constraints based on phonetics. See examples in [Kimball and Ostendorf, 1993] and [Digalakis and Murveit 1994].

Pronunciation Modeling   Individual HMMs for phones can be concatenated to model words. Linguistic knowledge, perhaps in the form of a dictionary or by rules, typically determines the sequence of phones that make up a word. Linguistic knowledge in the form of phonological rules can be used to model possible variations in pronunciation, such as the flap or stop realization of /t/. For computational efficiency (at the expense of storage), additional pronunciations can be added to the dictionary. This solution is not ideal for the linguist, since different pronunciations of the same word are treated as totally independent even though they may share all but one or two phones. It is also not an ideal engineering solution, since recognition accuracy may be lost depending on the implementation, since words with more pronunciations may be disfavored relative to those with few pronunciations. The work of Cohen (e.g. [Cohen et al., 1987]; Cohen, 1989) and others (see, e.g. [Withgott and Chen, 1993]) addresses some of these issues, but this area could likely benefit greatly from a better integration of symbolic knowledge with statistical models.

Language Modeling   Any method that can be used to constrain the sequences of occurring words can be thought of as a language model. Modeling sequences of words the way word pronunciations are typically modeled, (i.e., a dictionary of all possible pronunciations) is not a solution a linguist or an engineer would propose (except for the most constrained applications). A simple alternative is to model all words in parallel and add a loop from the end to the beginning, where one of the "words" is the "end-of-sentence" word so that the sentences are not infinitely long. Of course, this simple model has the disadvantage of assuming that the ends of all words are equivalent (the same state). This model assumes that at each point in an utterance, all words are equally likely, which is not true of any human language. Alternatively, Markov models can be used to estimate the likelihoods of words given the previous word (or N words or word classes), based on a training corpus of sentence transcriptions. Except for the intuition that some sequences are more likely than others, little linguistic knowledge is used. That intuition is difficult to call "linguistic" since, although there may be some recognition of doubtful cases, grammaticality has traditionally been a binary decision for many linguists. This will likely change as linguists begin to look at spontaneous speech data. Statistical modeling of linguistically relevant relationships (e.g., number agreement of subject and verb; or co-occurrences of adjectives with nouns, which may be an arbitrary number of words away from each other) is a growing area of interest. For examples, see the numerous papers on this topic in the (D)ARPA, Eurospeech, and International Conference on Spoken Language Processing (ICSLP) proceedings over the past several years.

Search Given the acoustic models, the language models, and the input speech, the role of the recognizer is to search through all possible hypotheses and find the best (most likely) string of words. As the acoustic and language models become more detailed they become larger, and this can be an enormous task, even with increasing computational power. Significant effort has been spent on managing this search. Recent innovations have involved schemes for making multiple passes using coarser models at first to narrow the search and progressively more detailed models to further narrow the pruned search space (see, e.g. [Murveit et al., 1993; Nguyen et al., 1993]). Typically, more extensive linguistic knowledge is more expensive to compute and is saved for later stages. The "N-best" approaches used for integration of speech and natural language (see section 5) have also been used to improve speech recognition.

4 Natural Language Understanding

Traditional approaches to NL understanding have been based in symbolic logic, using rule-based approaches typically involving large sets of handcrafted rules. However, since the first joint meeting of the speech and NL communities in 1989, the number of papers and the range of topics addressed using statistical methods have steadily increased. At the last two meetings, the category of statistical language modeling and methods received the most abstracts and was one of the most popular sessions.

In the merger of speech with NL, the traditional computational linguistic approach of covering a set of linguistically interesting examples was put to a severe test in the attempt to cover, in a limited domain, a set of utterances produced by people engaged in problem-solving tasks. Several new sources of complexity were introduced: the move to an empirically based approach (covering a seemingly endless number of "simple" things became more important than covering the "interesting," but more rare, complex phenomena), the separation of test and training materials (adding rules to cover phenomena observed in the training corpus may or may not affect coverage on an independent test corpus), the nature of spontaneous speech (which has a different, and perhaps more creative, structure than written language, previously the focus of much NL work), and recovery from errors that can occur in recognition or by the fact that talkers do not always produce perfectly fluent well-formed utterances. Many of the advantages of statistical approaches (as outlined above) are appropriate for dealing with these issues. The growing tendency to combine symbolic with statistical and engineering approaches, based on recent papers, is represented in several research areas described below.

Lexicon   Although speech recognition components usually use a lexicon, lexical tools in NL are more complex than lists of words and pronunciations. Different formalisms store different types and formats of information, including, for example, morphological derivations, part-of-speech information, and syntactic and semantic constraints on combinations with other words. Recently, there has been work in using statistical information in lexical work. See, for example, the use of sense-frequencies for word sense disambiguation in [Miller et al., 1994].

Grammar   An NL grammar has traditionally been a set of rules devised by observation of or intuitions concerning patterns in a language or sublanguage. Typically, such grammars have either accepted a sentence or rejected it, although grammars that degrade more gracefully in the face of spontaneous speech and recognition errors are being developed (see, e.g. [Hindle, 1992]). Based on the grammar used, the goal of parsing is to retrieve or assign a structure to a string of words for use by a later stage of processing. Traditionally, parsers have worked deterministically on a single string of input. When parsers were faced with typed input, aside from the occasional typographical error, the intended words were not in doubt. The merger of NL with speech recognition has forced NL components to consider speech disfluencies, novel syntactic constructions, and recognition errors. The indeterminancy of the input and the need to analyze various types of ill-formed input have led to an increased use of statistical methods. The (D)ARPA, Eurospeech, and ICSLP proceedings of recent years contain several examples of combining linguistic and statistical components in grammars, parsers, and part-of-speech taggers.

Interpretation   Interpretation is the stage at which a representation of meaning is constructed, and may occur at different stages in different systems. Of course, this representation is not of much use without a "back-end" that can use the representation to perform an appropriate response, for example, retrieve a set of data from a database, ask for more information, etc. This stage is typically purely symbolic, though likelihoods or scores of plausibility may be used. See also the work on sense disambiguation mentioned above. Some work has been devoted to probabilistic semantic grammars (see [Seneff, 1992]) and to "hidden understanding" (see [Miller, et al., 1995]).

5   Integration of Speech Recognition and Natural Language Understanding

The integration of speech with NL has several important advantages: (1) To NL understanding, speech recognition can bring prosodic information, information important for syntax and semantics but not well represented in text; (2) NL can bring to speech recognition several knowledge sources (e.g., syntax and semantics) not previously used (N-grams model only local constraints, and largely ignore systematic constraints such as number agreement); (3) for both, the integration affords the possibility of many more applications than could otherwise be envisioned, and the acquisition of new techniques and knowledge bases not previously represented.

Although there are many advantages, integration of speech and NL gives rise to some new challenges, including integration strategies, the effective use in NL of a new source of information from speech (prosody, in particular), and the handling of spontaneous speech effects. Prosody and disfluencies are especially important issues in the integration of speech and NL since the evidence for them is distributed throughout all linguistic levels, from phonetic to at least the syntactic and semantic levels. Integration strategies, prosody, and disfluencies are described briefly below (an elaboration appears in [Price, 1995]).

Integration   There is much evidence that human speech understanding involves the integration of a great variety of knowledge sources, and in speech recognition tighter integration of components has consistently led to improved performance. However, as grammatical coverage increases, standard NL techniques can become computationally difficult and provide less constraint for speech. On the other hand, a simple integration by concatenation is suboptimal because any speech recognition errors are propagated to the NL system and the speech system cannot take advantage of the NL knowledge sources. In the face of cultural and technical difficulties with tight integration and the limitations of a simple concatenation, "N-best" integration has become popular: The connection between speech and NL can be strictly serial, but fragility problems are mitigated by the fact that speech outputs not one but many hypotheses. The NL component can then use other knowledge sources to determine the best-scoring hypothesis. The (D)ARPA, Eurospeech, and ICSLP proceedings over the past several years contain several examples of the N-best approach. In addition, the special issue of *Speech Communication* on spoken dialogue [Shirai and Furui, 1994] contains several contributions on this topic.

Prosody *Prosody* can be defined as the suprasegmental information in speech; that is, information that cannot be localized to a specific sound segment, or information that does not change the segmental identity of speech segments. Prosodic information is not generally available in text-based systems, except insofar as punctuation may indicate some prosodic information. Prosody can provide information about syntactic structure, discourse, and emotion and attitude. A survey of combining statistical with linguistic methods in prosody appears in [Price and Ostendorf, 1995].

Spontaneous Speech The same acoustic attributes that indicate much of the prosodic structure (pitch and duration patterns) are also very common in aspects of spontaneous speech that seem to be more related to the speech planning process than to the structure of the utterance. Disfluencies are common in normal speech. However, modeling of speech disfluencies is only beginning (see [Shriberg et al., 1992; Lickley, 1994; Shriberg, 1994]). The distribution of disfluencies is not random, and may be a part of the communication itself. Although disfluencies tend to be less frequent in human-computer interactions than in human-human interactions, as people become increasingly comfortable with human-computer interactions and concentrate more on the task at hand than on monitoring their speech, disfluencies can be expected to increase.

6   Current Challenges

Although progress has been made in recent years in balancing symbolic with statistical methods in speech and language research, important challenges remain. A few of the challenges for speech recognition, for NL, and for their integration are outlined below.

6.1   Speech Recognition Challenges

Some of our knowledge, perhaps much of our knowledge, about speech has not been incorporated in automatic speech recognition systems. For example, the notion of a prototype and distance from a prototype (see, e.g. [Massaro, 1987; Kuhl, 1990]) which seems to explain much data from speech perception (and other areas of perception), is not well modeled in the current speech recognition frameworks. A person who has not been well understood tends to change his or her speech style so as to be better understood. This may involve speaking more loudly or more clearly, changing the phrasing, or perhaps even leaving pauses between words. These changes may help in human-human communication, but in typical human-machine interactions, they result in forms that are more difficult for the machine to interpret. The concept of a prototype in machine recognition could lead to more robust recognition technology.

That is, the maximum-likelihood approaches common in statistical methods to speech recognition miss a crucial aspect of language: the role of contrast. A given linguistic entity (e.g., phone) is characterized not just by what it is but also by what it is not, that is, the system of contrast in which it is involved. Thus, hyperarticulation may aid communication over noisy telephone lines for humans, but may decrease the performance of recognizers trained on a corpus in which this style of speech is rare or missing. The results can be disastrous for applications, since when a recognizer misrecognizes, a common reaction is to hyperarticulate ([Shriberg et al., 1992]).

Although many factors affect how well a system will perform, examining recent benchmark evaluations can give an idea of the relative difficulty of various aspects of speech (see e.g. [Pallett et al., 1995]). Such areas might be able to take advantage of increased linguistic knowledge. For example, the variance across the talkers used in the test set was greater than the variance across the systems tested. Further, the various systems tested had the highest error rates for the same three talkers, who were the fastest talkers in the set. These observations could be taken as evidence that variability in pronunciation, at least insofar as fast speech is concerned, is not yet well modeled.

6.2   Natural Language Challenges

Results in NL understanding have been more resistant to quantification than those in speech recognition; people agree more on what string of words was said than on what those words mean. Evaluation is important to scientific progress, but how do we evaluate an understanding system if we are unable to agree on what it means to understand? In the *DARPA* community, this question has been postponed somewhat by agreeing to evaluate on the answer returned from a database. Trained annotators examine the string of words (NL input) and use a database extraction tool to extract the minimum and maximum accepted set of tuples from the evaluation database. A "comparator" then automatically determines whether a given answer is within the minimum and maximum allowed.

The community is not, however, content with the current expense and limitations of the evaluation method described above, and is investing significant resources in finding a better solution. Key to much of the debate is the cultural gap: engineers are uncomfortable with evaluation measures that cannot be automated (forgetting the role of the annotator in the current process); and linguists are uncomfortable with evaluations that are not diagnostic; and, of course, neither side wants significant resources to go to evaluation that would otherwise go to research.

6.3   Integration Challenges

In fact, most of this chapter has addressed the challenge of integrating speech with NL, and much of the challenge has been argued to be related to cultural differences as much as to technical demands. As argued in Price and Ostendorf [1995], the increasingly popular classification and regression trees, or decision trees (see, e.g. [Breiman et al., 1984]) appear to be a particularly useful tool in bridging the cultural and technical gap in question. In this formalism, the speech researcher or linguist can specify the types of information that are known to affect variability (duration of a phone, for example), and based on a corpus of data in which these parameters are observed, the resulting tree can show how much of the variability is accounted for by each source of information (e.g., voicing of following consonant, compared to existence of following silence). Examples of the use of this tool are numerous: e.g. [Hirschberg, 1993; Ostendorf and Veilleux, 1993; Wang and Hirschberg, 1991; Withgott and Chen, 1993].

The advantages offered by multidisciplinary approaches are many, and there is more than one way to bridge two disciplines. One can become fluent in new areas and techniques, but this is increasingly difficult as the challenges of keeping up with existing fields increase. The gap can also be bridged by collaboration with others who are already fluent in the techniques, and by encouraging students to learn more about the techniques. The Balancing Act workshop was also an important vehicle in bridging the gap by bringing two communities together to focus on the topic.

Combining statistical with symbolic approaches has led to important gains in speech recognition and speech understanding, and to more powerful tools for acquiring further knowledge. Fuller understanding will require knowledge that spans all linguistic levels, from acoustics through semantics, pragmatics, and discourse. Few people are trained in all these areas. Fewer still have solid training in both statistical and symbolic methods. In the near term, multidisciplinary collaborations will likely be essential for rapid progress.

Acknowledgment

I thank Mari Ostendorf for her useful comments on the manuscript. I gratefully acknowledge the support of DARPA/ONR Contract ONR N00014-90-C-0085, and DARPA/NSF funding through NSF Grant IRI-8905249. The opinions expressed are mine and not necessarily those of the funding agencies.

References

Abrash, V., M. Cohen, H. Franco, and I. Arima (1994). Incorporating Linguistic Features in a Hybrid HMM/MLP Speech Recognizer. *Proceedings of the International Conference on Acoustics, Speech and Signal Processing*, 62.8.1–4.

Bahl, L., P. de Souza, P. Gopalakrishnan, D. Nahamoo, and M. Picheny (1991). Context Dependent Modeling of Phones in Continuous Speech using Decision Trees. *Proceedings of the DARPA Speech and Natural Language Workshop*, pp. 264–269.

Bahl, L., Jelinek, F. and Mercer, R. L. (1983). A Maximum Likelihood Approach to Continuous Speech Recognition. *IEEE Transactions on Pattern Analysis and Machine Intelligence PAMI-5, 2*, 179–190.

Breiman, L., J. H. Friedman, R. A. Olshen, and C. J. Stone (1984). *Classification and Regression Trees*. Monterey, Calif., Wadsworth and Brooks/Cole Advanced Books and Software.

Butzberger, J., H. Murveit, E. Shriberg, P. Price (1992). Spontaneous Speech Effects in Large Vocabulary Speech Recognition Applications. *Proceedings of the DARPA Speech and Natural Language Workshop*, pp. 339–343.

Cohen, M. (1989). *Phonological Structures for Speech Recognition*, Ph.D. thesis, Department of Computer Science, University of California at Berkeley, Ann Arbor, University of Michigan Microfilms.

Cohen, M., G. Baldwin, J. Bernstein, H. Murveit and M. Weintraub (1987). Studies for an Adaptive Recognition Lexicon. *Proceedings of the DARPA Speech and Natural Language Workshop*, pp. 49–55.

Digalakis, V., and H. Murveit (1994). An Algorithm for Optimizing the Degree of Tying in a Large Vocabulary Hidden Markov Model Based Speech Recognizer. *Proceedings of the International Conference on Acoustics, Speech and Signal Processing*, 54.2.1–4.

Hampshire, J., and A. Weibel (1990). Connectionist Architectures for Multi-Speaker Phoneme Recognition. In D. Rouretzky, editor. *Advances in Neural Information Processing Systems 2*, Morgan Kaufmann.

Hindle, D. (1992). An Analogical Parser for Restricted Domains. *Proceedings of the ARPA Human Language Technology Workshop*, pp. 150–154.

Hirschberg, J. (1993). Pitch Accent in Context: Predicting Prominence from Text. *Artificial Intelligence*, 63: 305–340.

Kimball, O., and M. Ostendorf (1993). On the Use of Tied-Mixture Distributions. *Proceedings of the ARPA Human Language Technology Workshop*, pp. 102–107.

Klatt, D. (1977). Review of the ARPA Speech Understanding Project. *Journal of the Acoustical Society of America*, 62: 1345–1366.

Kuhl, P. (1990). Towards a New Theory of the Development of Speech Perception. *Proceedings of the International Conference on Spoken Language Processing 2*, pp. 745–748.

Lickley, R. J. (1994). *Detecting Disfluency in Spontaneous Speech,* doctoral dissertation, University of Edinburgh, Scotland.

Massaro, D. (1987). *Speech Perception by Ear and Eye: A Paradigm for Psychological Inquiry,* Hillsdale, N.J., Erlbaum.

Miller, S., M. Bates, and R. Schwartz (1995). Recent Progress in Hidden Understanding Models. *Proceedings of the ARPA Human Language Technology Workshop,* pp. 276–280.

Miller, G. M. Chodorow, S. Landes, C. Leacock, and R. Thomas (1994). Using a Semantic Concordance for Sense Technology. *Proceedings of the ARPA Human Language Technology Workshop,* pp. 240–243.

Murveit, H., J. Butzberger, V. Digalakis, and M. Weintraub (1993). Large Vocabulary Dictation using SRI's DECIPHER Speech Recognition System: Progressive Search Techniques. *Proceedings of the International Conference on Acoustics, Speech and Signal Processing,* pp. II-319–322.

Nguyen, L., R. Schwartz, F. Kubala, and P. Placeway (1993). Search Algorithms for Software-Only Real-Time Recognition with Very Large Vocabularies. *Proceedings of the ARPA Human Language Technology Workshop* pp. 91–95.

Ostendorf, M., and S. Roukos (1989). A Stochastic Segment Model for Phoneme-Based Continuous Speech Recognition. *IEEE Transactions on Acoustics, Speech and Signal Processing,* December, pp. 1857–1869.

Ostendorf, M., and N. Veilleux (1994). A Hierarchical Stochastic Model for Automatic Prediction of Prosodic Boundary Location. *Computational Linguistics.* Vol. 20, No. 1, pp. 27–54.

Pallett, D. (1991). DARPA Resource Management and ATIS Benchmark Test Poster Session. *Proceedings of the Speech and Natural Language Workshop.* Morgan Kaufmann, pp. 49–58.

Pallett, D., N. Dahlgren, J. Fiscus, W. Fisher, J. Garofolo, and B. Tjaden (1992). DARPA February 1992 ATIS Benchmark Test Results. *Proceedings of the Speech and Natural Language Workshop,* San Mateo, Calif., Morgan Kaufmann, pp. 15–27.

Pallett, D., J. Fiscus, W. Fisher, and J. Garofolo (1993). Benchmark Tests for the DARPA Spoken Language Program. *Proceedings of the Human Language Technology Workshop,* San Francisco, Morgan Kaufmann, pp. 7–18.

Pallett, D., J. Fiscus, W. Fisher, J. Garofolo, B. Lund, and A. Martin, and M. Prysbocki (1995). 1994 Benchmark Tests for the ARPA Spoken Language Program. *Proceedings of the Human Language Technology Workshop.* Morgan Kaufmann, pp. 5–36.

Pallett, D., J. Fiscus, W. Fisher, J. Garofolo, B. Lund, and M. Prysbocki (1994). 1993 Benchmark Tests for the ARPA Spoken Language Program. *Proceedings of the Human Language Technology Workshop,* San Francisco, Morgan Kaufmann, in press.

Pallett, D., W. Fisher, J. Fiscus, and J. Garofolo (1990). DARPA ATIS Test Results. *Proceedings of the Speech and Natural Language Workshop.* Morgan Kaufmann, pp. 114–121.

Picone, J. (1990). Continuous Speech Recognition Using Hidden Markov Models. *IEEE ASSP Magazine*, pp. 26–41.

Price, P. (1995). Spoken Language Understanding. In R. Cole, J. Mariani, H. Uszkoreit, A. Zaenen, and V. Zue, editors. *Survey of the State of the Art in Human Language Technology.* Center for Spoken Language Understanding, Oregon Graduate Institute, pp. 48–55.

Price, P., and M. Ostendorf (1995). Combining Linguistic with Statistical Methods in Modeling Prosody. In J. L. Morgan and K. Demuth, editors, *Signal to Syntax: Bootstrapping from Speech to Grammar in Early Acquisition.* Hillsdale, N.J., Erlbaum.

Rabiner, L. (1989). A tutorial on hidden Markov models and selected applications in speech recognition. *IEEE Proceedings 77,* 2, 257–286.

Seneff, S. (1992). TINA, A Natural Language System for Spoken Language Applications. *Computational Linguistics,* 18: 61–86.

K. Shirai and S. Furui, guest editors. (1994). *Speech Communication.* Special Issue on Spoken Dialogue. 15. 3–4.

Shriberg, E., J. Bear, and J. Dowding (1992). Automatic Detection and Correction of Repairs in Human-Computer Dialog. *Proceedings of the DARPA Speech and Natural Language Workshop,* pp. 419–424.

Shriberg, E., E. Wade, and P. Price (1992). Human-Machine Problem Solving Using Spoken Language Systems (SLS): Factors Affecting Performance and User Satisfaction. *Proceedings of the DARPA Speech and Natural Language Workshop,* pp. 49–54.

Shriberg, E. E. (1994). *Preliminaries to a Theory of Speech Disfluencies,* doctoral dissertation, Stanford University, Stanford, Calif.

Stevens, K., S. Manuel, S. Shattuck-Hufnagel, and S. Liu (1992). Implementation of a Model for Lexical Access Based on Features. In *Proceedings of the 1992 International Conference on Spoken Language Processing,* Banff, vol. 1 pp. 499–502.

Wang, M., and J. Hirschberg (1991). Predicting Intonational Boundaries Automatically from Text: The ATIS Domain. *Proceedings of the DARPA Speech and Natural Language Workshop,* pp. 378–383.

Withgott, M., and F. Chen (1993). *Computational Models of American Speech.* CSLI Lecture Notes No. 32.

Zue, V., J. Glass, J. Goddeau, D. Goodine, L. Hirschman, H. Leung, M. Phillips, J. Polifroni, and S. Seneff (1992). The MIT ATIS System: February 1992 Progress Report. *Proceedings of the ARPA Human Language Technology Workshop,* pp. 84–88.

Chapter 7

Exploring the Nature of Transformation-Based Learning

Lance A. Ramshaw and Mitchell P. Marcus

Transformation-based, error-driven learning [Brill, 1993b] is a corpus-based method that has provided interesting results on a variety of tasks; the most notable of these is its application to part-of-speech tagging, owing to both the quality of the results and the existence of a publicly available implementation of the algorithm [Brill, 1995]. The overall approach can be distinguished from most other forms of corpus-based learning by its simplicity, and by the fact that it is based on counting but not on explicit probability estimates.

In "Exploring the Nature of Transformation-Based Learning," Ramshaw and Marcus provide a detailed investigation of the algorithm's properties— how it differs from statistical models based on explicit probability estimates such as hidden Markov models; how it relates to work in probabilistic machine learning such as decision trees; and why it exhibits less of a tendency to over-train than other supervised learning techniques. In the process, they elucidate their view of transformation-based learning as a "compromise method" involving both a statistical and a symbolic component. Crucially, and unlike most other hybrid approaches, the quantitative component of the algorithm makes its contribution only during training: the learner produces rules that are purely symbolic, interpretable, and modifiable.—Eds.

1 Introduction

Purely statistical methods like hidden Markov models (HMMs) have been applied with considerable success to linguistic problems like part-of-speech tagging. Recently, however, hybrid approaches have also begun to be explored that combine elements of symbolic knowledge with statistical learning algorithms. Such mixed models derive part of their power from the initial specification, determined by linguistic principles, of which factors should be included in the statistical search space. They also use representations that are more accessible to symbolic interpretation than is true of the purely statistical models. These models thus make it possible to bring linguistic knowledge to bear both in defining and tuning the model and in analyzing its results. This chapter focuses on transformation-based learning, which is one of these new compromise methods, and explores how it differs from existing, more purely statistical approaches.

Eric Brill in his thesis [Brill, 1993b] proposed "transformation-based error-driven learning" as a novel method for statistically deriving linguistic models from corpora. The technique has since been applied in various domains including part-of-speech tagging [Brill, 1992, 1994], building phrase structure trees [Brill, 1993a], text chunking [Ramshaw and Marcus, 1995], and resolving prepositional phrase attachment ambiguity [Brill and Resnik, 1994]. The method works by learning a sequence of symbolic rules that characterize important contextual factors and using those rules to predict a most likely value. The search for such factors only requires counting the instances of various sets of events that actually occur in a training corpus; the method is thus able to survey a larger space of possible contextual factors than could easily be captured by a statistical model that required explicit probability estimates for every possible combination of factors. Brill's results on part-of-speech tagging suggest that the method can achieve performance comparable to that of the HMM techniques widely used for that task, while also providing more compact and perspicuous models. Roche and Schabes [1995] have also shown that such models can be implemented as finite-state transducers whose speed is dominated by the access time of mass storage devices.

We have explored this new technique through a series of instrumented part-of-speech tagging experiments, using as data the tagged Brown Corpus [Francis and Kučera, 1979] and a tagged Septuagint Greek version of the first five books of the Bible [CATSS, 1991]. After briefly explaining the transformation-based learning approach and describing a new, fast implementation technique, this chapter uses the results of these tests to explore the differences between this technique and purely statistical models like HMMs. We also compare transformation-based learning with other partially symbolic methods like decision trees and decision lists, which are similar to it in that they survey a wide space of possible factors, initially identified using symbolic knowledge, in order to select factors to add to the model. These contrasts highlight the kinds of applications for which transformation-based learning is especially suited, and help to explain how it manages to largely avoid the difficulties with overtraining that affect the other approaches. We also describe a way of recording the dependencies between rules in the learned sequence that may be useful for further analysis.

2 Brill's Approach

As shown schematically in figure 7.1, transformation-based learning begins with a small, supervised training corpus, for which the correct tags are known. The first step is to use some "baseline" heuristic to select an initial current guess tag for each word (ignoring for the moment the known correct answers). In the part-of-speech tagging application, a plausible baseline heuristic might be to assign to each known word whose part of speech is ambiguous whatever tag is most often correct for that word in the training corpus, and to tag all unknown words as nouns. (Brill's results point out that performance on unknown words is a crucial factor for part-of-speech tagging systems. His system is therefore organized in two separate transformation-based training passes, with one important purpose of the first pass being exactly to predict the part of speech of unknown words. However, because the focus in these experiments is on understanding the mechanism rather than on comparative performance, the simple but unrealistic assumption of a closed vocabulary is made.)

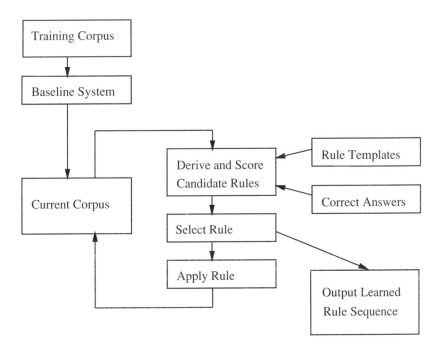

Figure 7.1
Learning a transformation-based model.

The method then learns a series of transformational rules that iteratively improve those initial baseline guesses. The space of possible rules that the algorithm searches is defined by a set of rule templates that select particular characteristics of particular words in the neighborhood of a given word as the grounds for changing the current tag at that location. For part-of-speech tagging, the rule templates typically involve either the actual words or the tags currently assigned to words within a few positions on each side of the location to be changed. The rule templates used in these experiments involve up to two of the currently assigned tags on each side of the tag being changed; they include [— C A/B — —] (change tag A to tag B if the previous tag is C) and [— — A/B C D] (change A to B if the following two tags are C and D). During training, instantiated rules like [— DET V/N — —] are built by matching these templates against the training corpus.

A set of such templates combined with the given part-of-speech tag set (and vocabulary, if the rule patterns also refer directly to the words) defines a large space of possible rules; the training process operates by using some ranking function to select at each step some rule judged likely to improve the current tag assignment. Brill suggests the simple ranking function of choosing (one of) the rule(s) that makes the largest net improvement in the current training set tag assignments. Note that applying a rule at a location can have a positive effect (changing the current tag assignment from incorrect to correct), a negative one (from correct to some incorrect value), or can be a neutral move (from one incorrect tag to another). Rules with the largest positive-minus-negative score cause the largest net benefit. In each training cycle, one such rule is selected and applied to the training corpus and then the scoring and selection process is repeated on the newly transformed corpus. This process is continued either until no beneficial rule can be found, or until the degree of improvement becomes less than some specified threshold. The process of scoring rule candidates is tractable despite the huge space of possible rules because rules that never apply positively can be ignored.

The final model is thus an ordered sequence of pattern-action rules. As shown in figure 7.2, it is used for prediction on a test corpus by beginning with the predictions of the baseline heuristic and then applying the transformational rules in order. In our test runs, seven templates were used during training to define the space of possible rules: three templates testing the tags of the immediate, next, and both neighbors to the left; three similar templates looking to the right; and a seventh template that tests the tags of the immediate left and right neighbors. The first 10 rules learned from a training run across a 50K-word

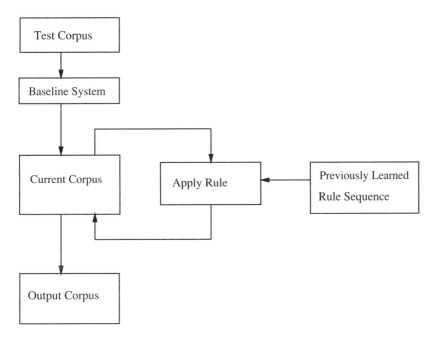

Figure 7.2
Applying a transformation-based model.

sample of the Brown Corpus are listed in figure 7.3; they closely replicate
Brill's original results [Brill, 1993b] allowing for the fact that his tests used
more templates, including templates like "if any one of the three previous tags
is A."

In later work, Brill [1994] improved the performance of his transformation-
based tagger by adding rule templates (not duplicated here) that were sensitive
not just to the tags of neighboring words but also to the actual lexical items
used, and by having the system learn a separate, initial set of rules to improve
the system's baseline guess as to the tag of words that never appeared in the
training data. His comparative results indicate that this approach can achieve a
level of performance on part-of-speech tagging that is at least on a par with that
of the HMM approaches that are frequently used [Jelinek, 1985; Church, 1988;
DeRose, 1988; Cutting et al., 1992], as well as showing promise for other
applications. The resulting model, encoded as a list of rules, is also typically
more compact and for many purposes more easily interpretable than a table of
HMM probabilities.

Pass			Rule			Pos.	Neg.	Neut.
1.	—	—	TO/IN	AT	—	227	0	0
2.	—	TO	NN/VB	—	—	113	13	0
3.	—	—	TO/IN	NN	—	49	0	0
4.	—	IN	PPS/PPO	—	—	51	4	0
5.	—	—	TO/IN	NP	—	46	0	0
6.	—	—	TO/IN	PP$	—	46	1	0
7.	—	—	CS/DT	NN	—	52	11	1
8.	—	HVD	VBD/VBN	—	—	38	0	0
9.	—	—	CS/QL	—	CS	41	7	0
10.	—	MD	NN/VB	—	—	32	0	0

Figure 7.3
First 10 rules learned on Brown Corpus sample.

3 An Incremental Algorithm

It is worthwhile noting first that it is possible in some circumstances to significantly speed up the straightforward algorithm described above. An improvement in our experiments of almost two orders of magnitude was achieved by using an incremental approach that maintains lists of pointers to link rules with the sites in the training corpus where they apply, rather than scanning the corpus from scratch each time. The improvement is particularly noticeable in the later stages of training, when the rules being learned typically affect only one or two sites in the training corpus. Note, however, that the linked lists in this incremental approach do require a significant amount of storage space. Depending on the number of possible rules generated by a particular combination of rule templates and training corpus, space constraints may not permit this optimization.

Incrementalizing the algorithm requires maintaining a list for each rule generated of those sites in the corpus where it applies, and a list for each site of the rules that apply there. Once one of the highest-scoring rules is selected, its list of site pointers is first used to make the appropriate changes in the current tag values in the corpus. After making the changes, that list is used again in order to update other rule pointers that may have been affected by them. It suffices to check each site within the span of the largest defined rule template from each changed site, testing to see whether all of its old rule links are still active, and whether any new rules now apply at that site. This algorithm is shown in figure 7.4. Note that after the initial setup it is only necessary to rescan the corpus when updating uncovers a rule that has not previously had any positive effect.

```
// Records for locations in the corpus, called "sites",
// include a linked list of the rules that apply at that site.
// Records for rules include score components (positive, negative, and neutral)
// and a linked list of the sites at which the rule applies.
// A hash table stores all rules that apply positively anywhere in the training.

scan corpus using templates, making hash table entries for positive rules
scan corpus again to identify negative and neutral sites for thos rules
loop
    high_rule := some rule with maximum score
    if high_rule.score ≤ 0
        then exit loop
    output rule trace
    for each change_site on high_rule.site_list do
        apply high_rule at change_site by changing current tag
    unseen_rules := ∅
    for each change_site on high_rule.site_list do
        for each test_site in the neighborhood of change_site do
            new_rules_list := NIL
            for each template do
                if template applies at test_site
                    then add resulting rule to new_rules_list
            for each rule in test_site.rules_list – new_rules_list do
                remove connection between rule and test_site
            for each rule in new_rules_list – test_site.rules_list do
                if rule in hash table
                    then make new connection between rule and test_site
                    else unseen_rules := unseen_rules ∪ {rule}
    If unseen_rules then ≠ ∅ then
        add unseen_rules to hash table
        for each site in corpus do
            for each rule in unseen_rules do
                if rule applies at site then
                    make connection between rule and site
                    adjust appropriate rule score (positive, negative, or neutral)
end loop
```

Figure 7.4
Incremental version of transformation-based learning algorithm.

4   The Effects of Iterative Transformations

Proceeding now to analysis of the method, many of the unusual features of transformation-based learning, when compared to methods like HMMs or decision trees, are directly related to its iterative character, that it learns rules not to assign tags de novo but to improve at each step on some current tag assignment. As we shall see in this section, this iterative character allows the technique to leverage new rules on the results of earlier ones. However, while this leveraging does provide a way for rules to interact with one another, the degree of that interaction is limited to that which can be mediated by current tag assignments. The iterative character of the method also plays a role in the analysis of different possible rule-ranking metrics and in explaining the limited amount of overtraining that this method seems to encounter.

It will frequently be helpful during the analysis to compare transformation-based learning with the more purely statistical HMM method, and with decision trees and decision lists. Decision trees [Breiman et al., 1984; Quinlan, 1993] are an established method for inducing quasi-symbolic, compact, and interpretable models. Black et al. [1992] have explored the use of decision trees for part-of-speech tagging, citing results that modestly outperformed an HMM model. If the occurrence of a particular tag in a given context is termed an *event*, their method constructed a decision tree with binary queries at each node that partitioned the set of events into leaves that were as indicative as possible of some particular tag. There are interesting similarities and differences between this approach and transformation-based learning. Yarowsky's use of decision lists for learning linguistic models [Yarowsky, 1993, 1994, 1995] results in a method which, like transformation-based learning, involves making selections from among a large number of possible rules or factors. However, while transformation-based learning works from a set of current guesses, choosing the rule that will most improve the score of the training set, and then repeating that process on the transformed corpus, the decision list technique is noniterative; it simply selects at each ambiguous site the single factor that provides the strongest evidence regarding the correct answer for that site.

4.1   Leveraging on Previous Rules

Some useful evidence for predicting the part of speech of a word in a corpus certainly comes from the identities of the neighboring words used within some window. However, it would also be useful to know the currently predicted tags for those neighboring words, since the tag-assignment problems for nearby words in a corpus are not independent. Since transformation-based learning is iterative, its rules can take account of the current best guesses for neighboring tags, and thus this method seems particularly well adapted to input that is inherently a sequence of such interrelated problem instances. Because the occurrence patterns for correct tags do depend in part on the unknown part-of-speech values at neighboring locations, it seems useful to allow the rule patterns to be based at each point on the system's best current guess for those values.

With HMM models [Rabiner, 1990], the Viterbi decoding procedure, which uses dynamic programming to efficiently determine the optimal path through the model, automatically allows the model's choice of tags at nearby locations to influence one another. In fact, that influence can be more fine-grained with HMMs than with transformation-based learning, since the HMM model is working with actual probability estimates rather than a single current best guess. However, because HMMs require a fully specified probabilistic model, they are typically more limited in terms of the contextual features represented.

Decision trees, on the other hand, are similar to transformation-based learning in being able to scan a large range of contextual features. However, they are traditionally applied to independent problem instances encoded as vectors of measurements for the various possibly relevant factors, and it is not clear in this approach how to allow the decisions at adjacent sites to influence each other. Black et al. [1992] included a leftward context of correct tags in their definition of the *events* from which their trees were learned, and thus their approach did allow for a one-way, left-to-right influence between sites. Magerman's decision-tree parser [Magerman, 1994, 1995] pushed that even further by exploring multiple paths through the decision space, and allowing each choice to depend on the choices that had been made so far along that particular path. However, it is difficult to exploit both leftward and rightward dependence when using decision trees, since changes in neighboring tag predictions could then force the recomputation of previous predicate splits higher in the tree.

Breaking the tag prediction process up into a series of rules that can each be applied immediately to the entire corpus is a simple scheme that allows the system to base its future learning on the improved estimates of neighborhood tags resulting from the operation of earlier rules. In a rule-based system without that sort of leverage, later rules would have to resolve an ambiguity at a neighboring location as part of a single rule pattern for the primary site, using as evidence only cases where the two occur together, while the iterative approach allows the system to use the best current guess for the neighboring site as part of the evidence for the choice at the primary site.

Intuitively, leveraging thus does appear to add significantly to the power of the rules. It remains an open question how much later rules in the sequences actually learned do depend on earlier ones, a point that is addressed further in section 5.

4.2   Limited Rule Dependence

While the iterative nature of this method does permit later rules to depend on the tag assignments made by earlier ones, that is the only way in which rules in the sequence can depend on one another, so that the overall character of the technique is still primarily one of independent rules. In this way, the approach is quite different from HMMs, for example, which construct a single mono-lithic model.

It is interesting to compare transformation-based learning in this regard with decision trees, since both employ models of similar granularity. In the building of a decision tree, an elementary predicate is selected at each step to split a for-mer leaf node, meaning that the new predicate is applied only to those training instances associated with that particular branch of the tree. The two new leaves thus created can be seen as embodying two new classification rules, each one covering exactly the subset of instances that classify to it; each rule's pattern thus includes all of the predicates inherited down that branch of the tree. In the transformation-based learning approach, on the other hand, new rules are gen-erated by applying the templates directly to the entire corpus. There is no cor-responding inheritance of earlier predicates down the branches of a tree; the only effect that earlier rules can have on later learning is through changing cur-rent tag assignments in the corpus.

It may be helpful in understanding this limited rule dependence mediated by tag assignments to consider a system where the rule templates would be tested each time against the current tag of the word to be changed, but where the rest of the rule pattern would be matched against the initial baseline tags at those loca-tions, rather than the current tags. Earlier rules could then affect later ones at a particular location only by changing the current tag assignment for that location itself. The firing of a rule at a location would make those rules that specify that new tag value as their central pattern element potentially applicable, while dis-abling those rules whose patterns specify the former tag; the training set at any time during training would thus in effect be partitioned for purposes of rule application into at most as many classes as there are tags. Such a system can be pictured as a lattice with one column for each tag assignment and with a single slanting arc at each generation that moves some corpus locations from one col-umn to another, an architecture that is reminiscent of the pylon structures used by Bahl et al. [1989] to represent the restricted forms of binary queries used in their decision tree approach to language modeling for speech recognition. While a path in a normal decision tree can encode an arbitrary amount of information in its branching, the paths in a transformation-based system must merge as often as they branch, restricting the amount of information that can be encoded and thus forcing the rules to be more independent.

Because of this limitation on transformation-based learning in terms of the connections between rules that can be constructed during training, any complex predicates that are going to be available must be built into the rule templates. A decision-tree learner, on the other hand, can be provided with elementary feature predicates; it will construct more complex combinations as it builds the tree. However, this additional power of decision-tree learners must be balanced against both their relative difficulty in taking account of dependence between ambiguities at neighboring sites and their constant fragmentation of the training set which, as noted below, appears to make them more subject to overtraining. If a transformation-based learner can be provided with an adequate initial set of templates, it has the advantages both of being sensitive to the mutual effects of tag choices at neighboring sites and of avoiding fragmentation of the training set.

4.3   Rule-Ranking Metrics

The iterative nature of transformation-based learning also means that alternative ranking metrics for selecting the best rule in each pass can significantly affect the path taken through the space of possible rule sequence models. The maximum net benefit metric that Brill proposes ranks rules by the improvement they cause on the training set, which is also the resubstitution estimate (a biased one) of the improvement that they would cause on the test set. That is certainly a reasonable choice, and if only one rule were going to be applied, it would be a very persuasive one. However, when selecting early rules in a sequence, it may be helpful to take into account that later rules will have the chance to try to fix any negative changes that this rule causes.

We thus explored a number of alternative metrics that seem to differ from the net benefit metric primarily in focusing more on rules that make many positive changes, and giving less weight to avoiding negative changes. We tried using likelihood ratio scores [Yarowsky, 1993; Dunning, 1993] and J-scores [Smyth and Goodman, 1992], as well as more ad hoc functions such as using a candidate rule's positive score minus some fraction of its negative score. However, while these alternative metrics did sometimes seem to produce better-performing rule sequences, we did not find differences large enough or consistent enough to justify any claim of superiority in general. We hope to continue to explore these matters further.

Different ranking metrics have also been proposed for choosing which leaves to split in decision trees. A simple approach that is similar to the net benefit metric is to choose on the basis of the immediate improvement in the score on the training set, but a number of other approaches have been explored that pay more attention to the distribution of items among the leaves, using either a diversity index or some information-theoretic measure based on the conditional entropy of the truth given the tree's predictions [Breiman et al., 1984; Buntine, 1992; Quinlan and Rivest, 1989; Quinlan, 1993]. Because successive splits in a decision tree can combine to synthesize a more complex predicate, each proposed split needs to be ranked partly with respect to what future splits it makes possible. It may even be useful to split a node in such a way that both of the new leaves would be assigned the same category as the parent; although such a rule does not change the training set score, it may make it easier for later rules to isolate particular subsets of those sites. In the transformation-based learning approach, however, a rule that did not change tags would have no effect, since earlier rules can only affect later ones by changing tags. This limited dependence between rules in transformation-based learning suggests that there would be less payoff here from a ranking metric that factored in the effect of each proposed rule on future rules.

4.4 Overtraining

One of the interesting features of transformation-based learning in comparison to other tagging models is a surprising degree of resistance to overtraining (or "overfitting"). For example, figure 7.5 shows the graph of percent correct on both the training set (*dotted line*) and the test set (*solid line*) as a function of the number of rules applied for a typical part-of-speech training run on 120K words of Greek text. The training set performance naturally improves monotonically, given the nature of the algorithm, but the surprising feature of that graph is that the test set performance seems to rise monotonically to a plateau, except for minor noise. This seems to be true for most of our transformation-based training runs, in marked contrast to similar graphs for decision trees or neural net classifiers or for the iterative EM training of HMM taggers on unsupervised data, where performance on the test set initially improves, but later significantly degrades.

Many of these learning methods typically encounter overtraining to an extent significant enough to motivate them to explore special techniques for controlling it. Schaffer [1993] usefully clarified the issues involved, pointing out that techniques to limit overtraining by pruning a decision tree or rule sequence are actually a form of bias in favor of simpler models. They are useful

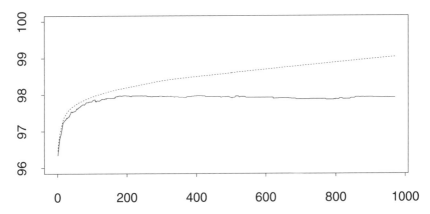

Figure 7.5
Training set (*dotted line*) and test set (*solid line*) performance on Greek corpus as a function of the number of rules applied.

exactly in those cases where the choice being predicted is likely to be in fact a fairly simple function of the measured features, but where the learning process is capable of exploring very complex models. The later stages of decision-tree training, for example, modify the model in ways that do make it fit the training set more closely, but which also, because it becomes a more complex model, make it inherently less likely to be true of text in general. Thus there is no one best technique for avoiding overtraining in general; the choice depends on the kinds of problems being modeled.

Within this context, the surprising fact about transformation-based learning is that the rule sequences learned typically do not experience significant overtraining. Experiments suggest that this is at least partly due to the knowledge embodied in the templates. When a part-of-speech training run is supplied with "relevant" templates, ones that identify significant and predictive tag patterns in the data, as in figure 7.5, one gets an "improve to plateau" test-set curve. "Irrelevant" templates, however, can lead to overtraining. Figure 7.6 shows that noticeable overtraining results from using just a single such template, in this case one that tested the tags of the words five positions to the left and right, which seem likely to be largely uncorrelated with the tag at the central location.

Figure 7.7, where this single irrelevant template is combined with the seven normal templates, shows that most of the overtraining in such cases happens late in the training process, when most of the useful relevant templates have already been applied. At that stage, as always, the templates are applied in each pass to each remaining incorrectly tagged site, generating candidate rules. Each

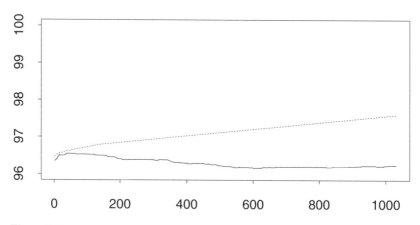

Figure 7.6
Training with one irrelevant template on Greek corpus.

rule naturally succeeds at the site that proposed it, but with respect to the rest of the training set, the changes proposed by rules at this stage are largely random, and are thus likely to do more harm than good when applied elsewhere, especially since most of the assigned tags in the corpus at this stage are correct. Thus if the rule's pattern matches elsewhere in the training set, it is quite likely that the effect there will be negative, so that the unhelpful rule will not be learned. Thus the presence of relevant templates supplies an important degree of protection against overtraining from any irrelevant templates, both by reducing the number of incorrect sites that are left late in training and by raising the percentage already correct, which makes it more likely that bad rules will be filtered out. The same applies, of course, to relevant and irrelevant instances of mixed templates, which is the usual case.

Most of the overtraining will thus come from patterns that match only once in the training set, to their generating instance. Under these assumptions, note that applying a score threshold greater than 1 can significantly reduce the overtraining risk, just as decision trees sometimes control that risk by applying a threshold to the entropy gain required before splitting a node. Brill's system uses a score threshold of 2 as the default, thus gaining additional protection against overtraining, while our experimental runs have been exhaustive, in order to better understand the mechanism.

Using test runs like those plotted above for irrelevant templates of various degrees of complexity, we also found a connection in terms of overtraining risk between the inherent matching probability of the templates used and the size of

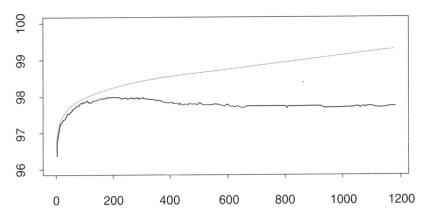

Figure 7.7
Training with seven relevant templates and one irrelevant template on Greek corpus.

the training set. A large training set means a larger number of incorrect sites that might engender overtrained rules, but also a better chance of finding other instances of those rule patterns and thus filtering them out. The combination of those factors appears to cause the risk of overtraining for a particular irrelevant template to first rise and then fall with increasing training set size, as the initial effect of increased exposure is later overcome by that of increased filtering from further occurrences of the patterns.

In comparing this with decision trees, the key contrast is that the filtering effect there decreases as training proceeds. The splitting predicates are applied to increasingly small fragments of the training set, so that the chance of filtering counterexamples also decreases. (With few points left in the region that the new rule will split, it becomes more likely that an irrelevant predicate will incorrectly appear to provide a useful split.) But since transformation-based learning continues to score its essentially independent rules against the entire training set, the protection of filtering against overtraining remains stronger.

It is worth adding that further experiments indicated that the degree of resistance of transformation-based learning to overtraining in these tests may be highly dependent on the degree of similarity between the training and test data. In the experiments reported above, the training and test data were separated by randomly selecting sentences, and, as mentioned before, the dictionary that was used was drawn from the entire corpus, including the test set, so that there also were no unknown words in the test material. In later tests, which did allow for unknown words or where the training and test material were not taken from the same corpus, it appeared that even training runs using relevant templates could encounter significant overtraining. Differences between training and test material both reduce the chance that positive changes in the training set will be reflected in the test set and also weaken the filtering effect which uses the training set to protect against rules that are likely to do harm on the test. These factors may explain why the resistance of transformation-based learning to overtraining is dependent on close similarity between the training and test data.

5 Tracking Rule Dependence

As noted earlier, since later rules in a sequence do sometimes depend on tag assignment changes made by earlier rules, it would be interesting to be able to characterize and quantify those rule dependencies. We have therefore added code that generates dependency trees showing the earlier rule applications (if any) that each rule depends on. For example, the dependency tree in figure 7.8 from the Brown Corpus data shows a case where the last rule that applied at this particular site (the bottom line in the figure, representing the root of the tree), which changed JJ to RB, depended on earlier rules that changed the previous site (relative position -1) to VBN and the following one (position +1) to DT. (The final number on each line tells on what pass that rule was learned. Also note that while recorded internally as trees, these structures actually represent dependency DAGs, since one rule application may be an ancestor of another along more than one path.)

All sites are initially assigned a null dependency tree representing the baseline heuristic choice. The application of a rule causes a new tree to be built, with a new root node, whose children are the current dependency trees for those locations referenced by the rule pattern. At the end of the training run, the final dependency trees for all the sites are sorted by size and structurally similar trees that show the same rules applied in the same relative pattern are grouped together. Those classes of trees are then sorted by frequency and output along with the list of rules learned.

+1:	—	—	CD/DT	NN	—	(7)
−1:	—	HVD	VBD/VBN	—	—	(8)
0:	—	VBN	JJ/RD	DT	—	(649)

Figure 7.8
Sample dependency tree from Brown Corpus data.

Certain common patterns of rule dependency can be noted in the resulting trees. A correction pattern results when one rule makes an overly general change, which affects not only appropriate sites but also inappropriate ones, so that a later rule in the sequence undoes part of the earlier effect. One example of this type from our Brown Corpus run can be seen in figure 7.9. Here the first rule was the more general one that changed PP$ to PPO whenever it follows VBD. While that rule was generally useful, it overshot in some cases, causing the later learning of a correction rule that changed PPO back to PP$ after RB VBD.

A chaining pattern occurs in cases where a change ripples across a context, as in figure 7.10. The first rule to apply here (21) changed QL to AP in relative position +2. That change enabled the RB to QL rule (181) at position +1, and together those two changes enabled the root rule (781). Note that this two-step rule chain has allowed this rule to depend indirectly on a current tag value that is further away than could be sensed in a single rule, given the current maximum template width.

This dependency tree output also shows something of the overall degree and nature of rule interdependence. The trees for a run on 50K words of the Brown Corpus bear out that rule dependencies, at least in the part-of-speech tagging application, are limited. Of a total of 3395 sites changed during training, only 396 had dependency trees with more than one node, and even the most frequent class of structurally similar trees appeared only four times. Thus the great majority of the learning in this case came from templates that applied in one step directly to the baseline tags, with leveraging being involved in only about 12% of the changes.

| 0: | — | VBD | PP$/PPO | — | — | (30) |
| 0: | RB | VBD | PPO/PP$ | — | — | (174) |

Figure 7.9
Sample correction-type dependency tree from Brown Corpus data.

+2:		—	—	QL/AP	CS	—	(21)
+1:	—	—	RB/QL	AP	CS		(181)
0:	—	—	NNS/VBZ	QL	AP		(781)

Figure 7.10
Sample chaining-type dependency tree from Brown Corpus data.

The relatively small amount of interaction found between the rules also suggests that the order in which the rules are applied may not be a major factor in
the success of the method for this particular application, and initial experiments
tend to bear this out. Figure 7.5 earlier showed the performance of a training
run on Greek text, where the rule to apply on each pass was selected using the
largest net benefit metric that Brill proposes. Note that, on this Greek corpus,
the initial baseline performance level of choosing the most frequent training set
tag for each word is already quite good; performance on both sets further
improves during training, with most of the improvement occurring in the first
few passes. In comparison, figure 7.11 shows the results for a training run
where the next rule at each step was randomly selected from among all rules
that had a net positive effect of any size. While the progress is more gradual,
both the training and test curves reach very close to the same maxima under
these conditions as they do when the largest net benefit rule is chosen at each
step. Note that it does take more rules to reach those levels, since the random
ranking presumably often ends up selecting more specific rules that are actually subsumed by more general ones not chosen till later. Thus at least for this
task, where there is little rule dependence, the choice of rule-ranking metric
does not seem to have much effect on the final performance achieved. The
largest net benefit ranking criterion is still a useful one, of course, if one wants
to find a short initial subsequence of rules that achieves the bulk of the
improvement.

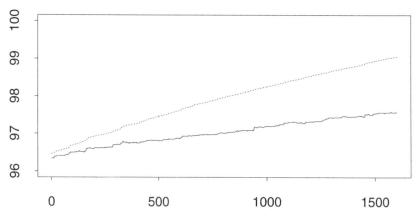

Figure 7.11
Training and test set performance on Greek, random-rule choice.

6 Future Work

The general analysis of transformation-based learning presented here is based on part-of-speech tagging experiments. Within that domain, it would be useful to quantify more clearly how transformation-based learning performs compared with other methods. It would be particularly interesting to see how it compares with traditional decision-tree methods when applied to the same corpora and making use of the same factors; such experiments would better illuminate the tradeoffs between the ability to combine predicates into more complex rules on the one hand and the ability to leverage partial results and resist overtraining on the other. It would also be useful to run tests similar to those presented here on overtraining risk and on rule dependence, using data from other domains, especially domains where the degree of rule dependence would be expected to be greater. Further exploration of the connections between transformation-based learning and decision trees and decision lists may also suggest other approaches, perhaps blends of the two, that would work better in some circumstances.

Within transformation-based learning itself, further work is required to determine whether other ranking schemes for selecting the next rule to apply might be able to improve on the simple maximum net benefit heuristic. It may also be possible to control for the remaining risk of overtraining in a more sensitive way than with a simple threshold. Selective pruning like that used with decision trees is one possible approach, and deleted estimation [Jelinek and Mercer, 1980] or other cross-validation techniques are also worth trying, though any technique that involves selecting particular rules from a sequence or merging two different sequences would have to deal with the hidden dependencies between rules. One goal for collecting the dependency tree data is to make it possible to prune or restructure rule sequences, using the recorded dependencies to maintain consistency among the remaining rules.

7 Conclusions

While transformation-based learning uses a simple, statistical search process to automatically select the rules in the rule-sequence model that it generates, symbolic linguistic knowledge also plays an important role. The fact that symbolic knowledge is required to specify the template patterns of relevant factors to be considered, as well as the fact that the resulting model is encoded as intelligible symbolic rules, makes this simple and powerful new mechanism for capturing the patterns in linguistic data an interesting compromise method to explore. The iterative nature of the approach turns out to be a key factor that sets it apart from other methods, in that it provides a limited way in which later rules can be leveraged on the results of earlier ones.

The technique has much in common with decision trees, especially in its ability to automatically select at each stage from a large space of possible factors the predicate or rule that appears to be most useful. One important difference is that decision trees can synthesize complex rules from elementary predicates by inheritance, while transformation-based learning must prespecify in the templates essentially the full space of possible rules. However, as long as the template set can be made rich enough to cover the patterns likely to be found in the data, this restriction in power may not cause too great a reduction in performance, and it brings two important benefits in return: first, breaking the model up into independent rules makes it possible to apply them to the whole corpus as they are learned, allowing the rules to leverage off the best estimates regarding their surroundings; and second, since the independent rules continue to be scored against the whole training corpus, a substantial measure of protection against overtraining is gained.

References

Bahl, Lalit R., Peter F. Brown, Peter V. de Souza, and Robert L. Mercer. 1989. A tree-based statistical language model for natural language speech recognition. *IEEE Transactions on Acoustics, Speech, and Signal Processing,* 37: 1001–1008.

Black, Ezra, Fred Jelinek, John Lafferty, Robert Mercer, and Salim Roukos. 1992. Decision tree models applied to the labeling of text with parts-of-speech. In *Speech and Natural Language Workshop Proceedings,* pp. 117–121. Morgan Kaufmann, San Mateo, Calif.

Breiman, Leo, Jerome H. Friedman, Richard A. Olshen, and Charles J. Stone. 1984. *Classification and Regression Trees.* Pacific Grove, Calif., Wadsworth & Brooks/Cole.

Brill, Eric. 1992. A simple rule-based part of speech tagger. In *Proceedings of the DARPA Speech and Natural Language Workshop, 1992.*

Brill, Eric. 1993a. Automatic grammar induction and parsing free text: a transformation-based approach. In *Proceedings of the DARPA Speech and Natural Language Workshop, 1993,* pp. 237–242.

Brill, Eric. 1993b. *A Corpus-Based Approach to Language Learning.* Ph.D. thesis, University of Pennsylvania, Philadelphia.

Brill, Eric. 1994. Some advances in transformation-based part of speech tagging. In *Proceedings of the Twelfth National Conference on Artificial Intelligence,* pp. 722–727.

Brill, Eric. Transformation-based tagger, version 1.14. ftp://blaze.cs.jhu.edu/pub/brill/Programs/RULE_BASED_TAGGER_V.1.14.tar.Z, 1995.

Brill, Eric and Philip Resnik. 1994. A rule-based approach to prepositional attachment disambiguation. In *Proceedings of the Sixteenth International Conference on Computational Linguistics,* Association for Computational Linguistics, Morristown, NJ.

Buntine, Wray. 1992. Learning classification trees. *Statistics and Computing,* 2: 63–73.

CATSS. 1991. Produced by Computer-Assisted Tools for Septuagint Studies, available through the University of Pennsylvania's Center for Computer Analysis of Texts.

Church, Kenneth. 1988. A stochastic parts program and noun phrase parser for unrestricted text. In *Second Conference on Applied Natural Language Processing.* Association for Computational Linguistics, Morristown, NJ.

Cutting, D., J. Kupiec, J. Pederson, and P. Sibun. 1992. A practical part-of-speech tagger. In *Proceedings of the Third Conference on Applied Natural Language Processing.* Association for Computational Linguistics, Morristown, NJ.

DeRose, Steven J. 1988. Grammatical category disambiguation by statistical optimization. *Computational Linguistics,* 14: 31–39.

Dunning, Ted. 1993. Accurate methods for the statistics of surprise and coincidence. *Computational Linguistics,* 19: 61–74.

Francis, W. Nelson and Henry Kučera. 1979. *Manual of Information to Accompany a Standard Corpus of Present-Day Edited American English, for use with Digital Computers.* Technical Report. Providence, R.I., Department of Linguistics, Brown University.

Jelinek, F. 1985. Markov source modeling of text generation. In J. K. Skwirzynski, editor, *The Impact of Processing Techniques on Communication.* Dordrecht, Nijhoff.

Jelinek, F. and R. L. Mercer. 1980. Interpolated estimation of Markov source parameters from sparse data, pp. 381–397. In E. S. Gelsema and L. N. Kanal, editors, *Pattern Recognition in Practice.* Amsterdam, North-Holland.

Magerman, David M. 1994. *Natural Language Parsing as Statistical Pattern Recognition,* Ph.D. thesis, Stanford University, Stanford, Calif.

Magerman, David M. 1995. Statistical decision-tree models for parsing. In *Proceedings of the 33rd Annual Meeting of the Association for Computational Linguistics,* Morristown, NJ, pp. 276–283.

Quinlan, J. Ross. 1993. *C4.5: Programs for Machine Learning.* San Francisco, Calif., Morgan Kaufmann.

Quinlan, J. Ross, and Ronald L. Rivest. 1989. Inferring decision trees using the minimum description length principle. *Information and Computation,* 80: 227–248.

Rabiner, Lawrence R. 1990. A tutorial on hidden Markov models and selected applications in speech recognition. In Alex Waibel and Kai-Fu Lee, editors, *Readings in Speech Recognition.* Los Altus, Calif., Morgan Kaufmann. Originally published in *Proceedings of the IEEE* in 1989.

Ramshaw, Lance A. and Mitchell P. Marcus. 1995. Text chunking using transformation-based learning. In *Proceedings of the ACL Third Workshop on Very Large Corpora,* pp. 82–94.

Resnik, Philip S. 1993. *Selection and Information: A Class-Based Approach to Lexical Relationships.* Ph.D. thesis. Philadelphia, University of Pennsylvania, Philadelphia, Institute for Research in Cognitive Science Report No. 93–42.

Roche, Emmanuel and Yves Schabes. 1995. Deterministic part-of-speech tagging with finite-state transducers. *Computational Linguistics,* 21: 227–253.

Schaffer, Cullen. 1993. Overfitting avoidance as bias. *Machine Learning,* 10: 153–178.

Smyth, Padhraic and Rodney Goodman. 1992. An information theoretic approach to rule induction from databases. *IEEE Transactions on Knowledge and Data Engineering,* 4: 301–316.

Weischedel, Ralph, Marie Meteer, Richard Schwartz, Lance Ramshaw, and Jeff Palmucci. 1993. Coping with ambiguity and unknown words through probabilistic methods. *Computational Linguistics,* 19: 359–382.

Yarowsky, David. 1993. One sense per collocation. In *Human Language Technology, Proceedings of the DARPA Workshop,* pp. 266–277. San Francisco, Morgan Kaufmann.

Yarowsky, David. 1994. Decision lists for lexical ambiguity resolution: Application to accent restoration in Spanish and French. In *Proceedings of the 32th Annual Meeting of the Association for Computational Linguistics,* pp. 88–95.

Yarowsky, David. 1995. Unsupervised word sense disambiguation rivaling supervised methods. In *Proceedings of the 33rd Annual Meeting of the Association for Computational Linguistics,* pp. 189–196.

Chapter 8

| Recovering from Parser Failures: A Hybrid Statistical and Symbolic Approach | Carolyn Penstein Rosé and Alex H. Waibel |

Most linguistic analyses assume an ideal speaker-hearer, who will utter only grammatical sentences or grammatical sentence fragments. But spontaneous speech is full of extragrammatical phenomena, such as false starts, words not listed in the lexicon, and ungrammatical constructions. Although it is unclear whether this type of data should be accounted for in a linguistic theory, there is no question that the computational linguist needs to account for such possibilities. Similarly, the question of whether such data falls inside the purview of a linguistic theory of competence or only in a performance model is debatable (see Abney, chapter 1).

Rosé and Waibel provide a detailed system description of an approach to recovering from parser failures that builds on an effective hybrid model. The repair module uses symbolic information as the basis of the feature-structure conceptual representation built during analysis from input into interlingua. Statistical information is used to optimize the computation of ways partial analyses can fit together to create a valid structure for input into the interlingua. Rosé and Waibel argue that by drawing upon both statistical and symbolic sources of information, the repair module can constrain its repair predictions to those which are both likely (a statistical notion) and meaningful (a symbolic notion). The complete description of their working system, along with evaluation of results, provides a convincing example of the effectiveness of balancing approaches.—Eds.

1   Introduction

Natural language processing of spontaneous speech is particularly difficult because it contains false starts, out-of-vocabulary words, and ungrammatical constructions. Because of this, it is unreasonable to hope to be able to write a grammar that will cover all of the phenomena that a parser is likely to encounter in a practical speech translation system. In this chapter we describe an implementation of a hybrid statistical and symbolic approach for recovering from parser failures in the context of a speech-to-speech translation system of significant scope (vocabulary size of 996, word recognition accuracy 60%, grammar size on the order of 2000 rules). The domain which the current system focuses on is the scheduling domain where two speakers attempt to set up a meeting over the telephone.

Because this is an interlingua-based translation system, the goal of the analysis stage of the translation process is to map the utterance in the source language onto a feature-structure representation called an interlingua which represents meaning in a language-independent way. If the parser cannot derive a complete analysis for an utterance, it derives a partial parse by skipping over portions of the utterance in order to find a subset which can parse. It also returns an analysis for the skipped portions which can be used to rebuild the meaning of the input utterance. The goal of the repair module is to interactively reconstruct the meaning of the full utterance by generating predictions about the way the fragments can fit together and checking them with the user. In this way it negotiates with the user in order to recover the meaning of the user's utterance.

The repair module described in this chapter uses both symbolic and statistical information to reconstruct the speaker's meaning from the partial analysis which the parser produces. It generates predictions based on constraints from a specification of the interlingua representation and from mutual information statistics extracted from a corpus of naturally occurring scheduling dialogues. Mutual information is intuitively a measure of how strongly associated two concepts are.

Although the syntactic structure of the input utterance certainly plays an important role in determining the meaning of an utterance, it is possible with the use of the interlingua specification to reason about the meaning of an utterance when only partial structural information is available. This can be accomplished by fitting the partial feature structures together against the mold of the interlingua specification. During the parsing process, two structural representations are generated: one is a treelike structure generated from the structure of the context-free portion of the parsing grammar rules; the other is a feature-structure generated from the unification portion of the parsing grammar rules. There is a many-to-one mapping between tree-structures and feature-structures. Both of these structures are important in the repair process.

The repair process is analogous in some ways to fitting pieces of a puzzle into a mold that contains receptacles for particular shapes. The interlingua specification is like the mold with receptacles of different shapes, making it possible to compute all of the ways partial analyses can fit together in order to create a structure that is valid for the given interlingua. But the number of ways it is possible to do this are so numerous[1] that the brute force method is computationally intractable. Mutual information statistics are used to guide the search. These mutual information statistics encode regularities in the types of fillers which tend to occur in particular slots and which feature-structures associated with particular non-terminal symbols in the parsing grammar tend to be used in a particular way in the interlingua representation. By drawing upon both statistical and symbolic sources of information, the repair module can constrain its repair predictions to those which are both likely and meaningful.

One advantage of the design of this module is that it draws upon information sources that were already part of the system before the introduction of the repair module. Most of the additional information which the module needs was trained automatically using statistical techniques. The advantage of a design is that the module can be easily ported to different domains with minimal additional effort. Another strength is that the statistical model the repair module makes use of continually adapts during use. This is desirable in a statistical approach in order to overcome problems with unbalanced training sets or training sets that are too small, leading to overfitting.

2 Motivation

The overwhelming majority of research in symbolic approaches to handling ill-formed input has focused on flexible parsing strategies. Hobbs and co-workers [2], McDonald [5], Carbonell and Hayes [1], Ward and co-workers [6], Lehman [4], and Lavie and Tomita [3] have all developed types of flexible parsers. Hobbs et al. and McDonald each employ grammar-specific heuristics which are suboptimal since they fall short of being completely general. Ward and Carbonell take a pattern-matching approach which is not specific to any particular grammar but the structure of the output representation is not optimal for an application where the output representation is distinct from the structure of the parse, for example, a feature-structure, as in an interlingua-based machine translation system.

Both Lehman and Lavie take an approach that is independent of any particular grammar and makes it possible to generate an output representation distinct from the structure of the parse. Lehman's least-deviant-first parser can accommodate a wide range of repairs of parser failures. But, as it adds new rules to its grammar in order to accommodate idiosyncratic language patterns, it quickly becomes intractable for multiple users. Also, because it does not

---

1. The search space is theoretically infinite since the interlingua representation is recursive.

make use of any statistical regularities, it has to rely on heuristics to determine which repair to try first. Lavie's approach is a variation on Tomita's Generalized LR parser, which can identify and parse the maximal subset of the utterance that is grammatical according to its parsing grammar. He uses a statistical model to rank parses in order to deal with the extraordinary amount of ambiguity associated with flexible parsing algorithms. His solution is a general one. The weakness of this approach is that part of the original meaning of the utterance may be thrown away with the portions of the utterance that were skipped in order to find a subset which can parse.

From a different angle, Gorin [2] has demonstrated that it is possible to successfully build speech applications with a purely statistical approach. He makes use of statistical correlations between features in the input and the output which purely symbolic approaches do not in general make use of. The evidence provided by each feature combines in order to calculate the output which has the most cumulative evidence. In Gorin's approach, the goal is not to derive any sort of structural representation of the input utterance. It is merely to map the set of words in the input utterance onto some system action. If the goal is to map the input onto a meaning representation, as is the case in an interlingua-based machine translation project, the task is more complex. The set of possible meaning representations, even in a relatively small domain such as scheduling, is so large that such an approach does not seem practical in its pure form. But if the input features encode structural and semantic information, the same idea can be used to generate repair hypotheses.

The repair module described in this chapter builds upon Lavie and Tomita's and Gorin's approaches, reconstructing the meaning of the original utterance by combining the fragments returned from the parser, and making use of statistical regularities to naturally determine which combination to try first. In our approach we have attempted to abstract away from any particular grammar in order to develop a module that can be easily ported to other domains and other languages. Our approach allows the system to recover from parser failures and adapt without adding any extra rules to the grammar, allowing it to accommodate multiple users without becoming intractable.

The repair module was tested on two corpora with 129 sentences each. One corpus contains 129 transcribed sentences from spontaneous scheduling dialogues. These sentences were transcribed just as they were spoken, so they contain all of the false starts and ungrammaticalities of natural speech. The other corpus contains the output from the speech recognizer from reading the transcribed sentences. So it contains all of the difficulties of the transcribed corpus in addition to speech recognition errors. Given a maximum of 10 questions to ask the user, it can raise the accuracy of the parser (point value derived from automatically comparing generated feature-structures to hand-coded ones) from 52% to 64% on speech data and from 68% to 78% on transcribed data. Given a maximum of 25 questions, it can raise the accuracy to 72% on speech data and 86% on transcribed data.

3 Symbolic Information

The system which this repair module was designed for is an interlingua-based machine translation system. This means that the goal of the analysis stage is to map the input utterance onto a language-independent representation of meaning called an interlingua. Currently, the parsing grammar that is used is a semantic grammar which maps the input utterance directly onto the interlingua representation. Although the goal of an interlingua is to be language-independent, most interlinguas are domain-dependent. Although this may seem like a disadvantage, it actually makes it possible for domain knowledge to be used to constrain the set of meaningful interlingua structures for that domain, which is particularly useful for constraining the set of possible repairs that can be hypothesized. The domain which the current system focuses on is the scheduling domain where two speakers attempt to set up a meeting over the phone.

The interlingua is a hierarchical feature-structure representation. Each level of an interlingua structure contains a frame name which indicates which concept is represented at that level, such as *busy or *free. Each frame is associated with a set of slots which can be filled either by an atomic value or by another feature-structure. At the top level, additional slots are added for the sentence type and the speech act. Sentence type roughly corresponds to mood, that is, *state is assigned to declarative sentences and *query-if is assigned to yes/no questions. The speech act indicates what function the utterance performs in the discourse context. (See the sample interlingua structure in figure 8.1.)

```
((speech-act (*multiple*
             *state-constraint *reject))
 (sentence-type *state)
 (frame *busy)
 (who ((frame *i)))
 (when
     ((frame *special-time)
      (next week)
      (specifier (*multiple* all-range
                 next)))))
```

Figure 8.1
Sample interlingua representation returned by the parser for "I'm busy all next week."

The interlingua specification determines the set of possible interlingua structures. This specification is one of the key symbolic knowledge sources used for generating repair hypotheses. It is composed of BNF-like rules which specify subsumption relationships between types of feature-structures (figure 8.2), or between types of feature-structures and feature-structure specifications (figure 8.3).

A feature-structure specification is a feature-structure whose slots are filled in with types rather than with atomic values or feature-structures. Feature-structure specifications are the leaves of the subsumption hierarchy of interlingua specification types. Because the interlingua representation is defined independently of the repair module, this approach extends to other feature-structure–based meaning representations as well.

$$(<TEMPORAL> = <SIMPLE - TIME>$$
$$<INTERVAL>$$
$$<SPECIAL - TIME>$$
$$<RELATIVE - TIME>$$
$$<EVENT - TIME>$$
$$<TIME - LIST>)$$

Figure 8.2
Sample interlingua specification rule for expressing a subsumption relationship between type $<TEMPORAL>$ and more specific temporal types.

$$(<BUSY> = ((\text{frame *busy})$$
$$(\text{topic } <FRAME>)$$
$$(\text{who } <FRAME>)$$
$$(\text{why } <FRAME>)$$
$$(\text{when } <TEMPORAL>)$$
$$(\text{how-long } <LENGTH>)$$
$$(\text{degree [DEGREE]})))$$

Figure 8.3
Sample interlingua specification rule for expressing a subsumption relationship between the type $<BUSY>$ and the feature-structure specification for the frame *busy.

4   Statistical Knowledge

Intuitively, repair hypotheses are generated by computing the mutual information between semantic grammar non-terminal symbols and types in the interlingua specification and also between slot-type pairs and types that are likely to be fillers of that slot. Mutual information is roughly a measure of how strongly associated two concepts are. It is defined by the following formula:

$$log[P(c_k \mid v_m)/P(c_k)]$$

where c_k is the kth element of the input vector and v_m is the mth element of the output vector.

Based on Gorin's approach, statistical knowledge in our repair module is stored in a set of networks with weights corresponding to the mutual information between an input unit and an output unit. Gorin's network formalism is appealing because it can be trained both off-line with examples and on-line during use. Another positive aspect of Gorin's mutual information network architecture is that rather than provide a single hypothesis about the correct output, it provides a ranked set of hypotheses, so if the user indicates that it made the wrong decision, it has a natural way of determining what to try next. It is also possible to introduce new input units at any point in the training process. This allows the system to learn new words during use which will be explained in more detail below. In the limit, this gives the system the additional ability to handle nil parses.

Our implementation of the repair module has code for generating and training five instantiations of Gorin's network architecture, each used in a different way in the repair process.

The first network is used for generating a set of hypothesized types for chunks with feature-structures that have no type in the interlingua specification. The parse associated with these chunks is most commonly a single symbol dominating a single word. This occurs when the parser skips over a word or set of words which cannot be parsed into a feature structure covered by the interlingua specification, as is the case with unknown words. The symbol is used to compute a ranked set of likely types the symbol is likely to map onto based on how much mutual information it has with each output node. In the case that this is a new symbol which the net has no information about yet, it will return a ranked list of types based on how frequently those types are the correct output. This effect falls naturally out of the activation function. Activation of an output node is calculated by summing the mutual information between each of the activated input nodes and the output node in question. Finally a bias is added, which is the proportion of iterations in which the output node in question was selected as the correct output node during training. Because a new symbol will have the same mutual information with each of the output nodes, the only thing that will distinguish one from another is the bias.

The second network is used for calculating what types are likely fillers for particular frame slot pairs, for example, a slot associated with a particular frame. This is used for generating predictions about likely types of fillers which could be inserted in the current interlingua structure. This information can help the repair module interpret chunks with uncertain types in a top-down fashion.

The third network is similar to the first network except that it maps collections of parser non-terminal symbols onto types in the interlingua specification. It is used for guessing likely top-level semantic frames for sentences and for building larger chunks out of collections of smaller ones.

The fourth network is similar to the third except instead of mapping collections of parser non-terminal symbols onto types in the interlingua specification, it maps them onto sentence types (see discussion on interlingua representation). This is used for guessing the sentence type after a new top-level semantic frame has been selected.

The fifth and final network maps a boolean value onto a ranked set of frame slot pairs. This is used for generating a ranked list of slots that are likely to be filled. This network complements the second network. A combination of these two networks yields a list of slots likely to be filled along with the types they are likely to be filled with.

Our implementation of the mutual information networks allows for a mask to filter out irrelevant hypotheses so that only the outputs that are potentially relevant at a given time will be returned.

5 The Repair Process: Detailed Description

In this section we give a detailed high-level description of the operation of the Repair Module.

5.1 System Architecture

The heart of the Repair Module (figure 8.4) is the Hypothesis Generation Module whose purpose it is to generate repair hypotheses, which are instructions for reconstructing the speaker's meaning by performing operations on the Chunk Structure of the parse. The Chunk Structure represents the relationships between the partial analysis and the analysis for each skipped segment of the utterance (see figure 8.5).

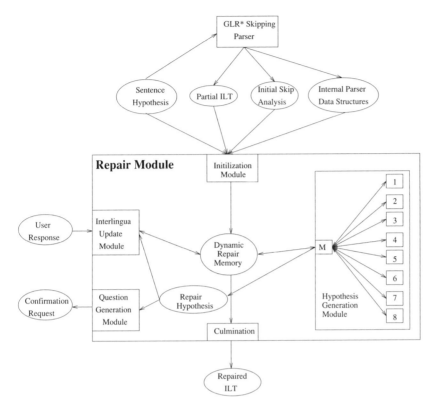

Figure 8.4
Repair module system architechture.

The Initialization Module builds this structure from the fragmented analysis returned by the parser. It inserts this structure into the Dynamic Repair Memory structure which serves as a blackboard for communication between modules. The Dynamic Repair Memory also contains slots for the current repair hypothesis and the status of that hypothesis, that is, test, pass, fail. There are essentially four types of repair hypotheses that the Hypothesis Generation Module can generate. These are guessing the top-level semantic frame for the interlingua structure of the sentence, guessing the sentence type, combining chunks into larger chunks, and inserting chunks into the current interlingua structure.

The Hypothesis Generation Module has access to eight different strategies for generating repair hypotheses. The strategy determines which of the four types of hypotheses it should generate on each iteration. A meta-strategy selects which strategy to employ in a given case.

Speaker's Utterance: *Tuesday afternoon the ninth would be okay for me though.*

Speech Hypothesis From the Recognizer: Tuesday afternoon the ninth be okay for me that.

Partial Analysis:

((sentence-type *fragment)
(when ((frame *simple-time)
    (time-of-day afternoon)
    (day-of-week Tuesday)
    (day 9)))

Paraphrase of partial analysis: Tuesday afternoon the ninth

Skipped Portions:

1. ((value be))
2. ((frame *free) (who ((frame *i))) (good-bad +))
3. ((frame *that))

Figure 8.5
Sample partial parse.

Once the hypothesis is generated, it is sent to the Question Generation Module which generates a question for the user to check whether the hypothesis is correct. After the user responds, the status of the hypothesis is noted in the Dynamic Repair Memory and if the response was positive, the Interlingua Update Module makes the specified repair and updates the Dynamic Repair Memory structure. It is the Interlingua Update Module which uses these hypotheses to actually make the repairs to derive the complete meaning representation for the utterance from the partial analysis and the analysis for the skipped portions.

If the status indicates that the speaker's response was negative, the Hypothesis Generation Module will suggest an alternative repair hypothesis which is possible since the mutual information nets return a ranked list of predictions rather than a single one. In this way the repair module negotiates with the speaker about what was meant until an acceptable interpretation can be constructed (figure 8.6). When the goal returns positive, the networks are reinforced with the new information so they can improve their performance over time.

5.2   The Three Questions

The eight strategies are generated by all possible ways of selecting either top-down or bottom-up as the answer to three questions.

Interlingua Representation:
((sentence-type *state)
(frame *free)
(who ((frame *i)))
(when ((frame *simple-time)
    (time-of-day afternoon)
    (day-of-week Tuesday)
    (day 9))))
Paraphrase: I am free Tuesday afternoon the ninth.

Figure 8.6
Complete meaning representation after repair.

The first question is, "What will be the top-level semantic frame?" The top-down approach is to keep the partial analysis returned by the parser as the top-level structure, thereby accepting the top-level frame in the partial analysis returned by the parser as representing the gist of the meaning of the sentence. Strategies 1 through 4 use the top-down approach. The bottom-up approach is to assume that the partial analysis returned by the parser is merely a portion of the meaning of the sentence which should fit into a slot inside of some other top-level semantic frame. This is the case in the example in figure 8.5. Strategies 5 through 8 use the bottom-up approach. If bottom-up is selected, a new top-level semantic frame is chosen by taking the set of all parser non-terminal symbols in the tree-structure for the partial analysis from each skipped segment and computing the mutual information between that set and each interlingua specification type. This gives it a ranked set of possible types for the top-level interlingua structure. The interlingua specification rule for the selected type would then become the template for fitting in the information extracted from the partial analysis as well as from the skipped portions of the utterance (figure 8.7). If a new top-level frame was guessed, then a new sentence type must also be guessed. Similar to guessing a top-level frame, it computes the mutual information between the same set of parser non-terminal symbols and the set of sentence types.

The second question is, "How will constituents be built?" The top-down approach is to assume that a meaningful constituent to insert into the current interlingua structure for the sentence can be found by simply looking at available chunks and portions of those chunks (figure 8.8). Strategies 1, 2, 5, and 6 use the top-down approach. The bottom-up approach is to assume that a

Question: What will be the top-level structure?
Answer: Try Bottom-Up.
Hypothesis: (top-level-frame ((frame-name *free)))
Question: Is your sentence mainly about someone being free?
User Response: *Yes.*
New Current Interlingua Structure:
((frame *free))
Skipped Portions:
1. ((value be))
2. ((frame *free) (who ((frame *i))) (good-bad +))
3. ((frame *that))
4. ((frame *simple-time) (time-of-day afternoon) (day-of-week Tuesday) (day 9))

Figure 8.7
The first question.

meaningful chunk can be constructed by combining chunks into larger chunks which incorporate their meaning. The process of generating predictions about how to combine chunks into larger chunks is similar to guessing a top-level frame from the utterance except that only the parser non-terminal symbols for the segments in question are used to make the computation. Strategies 3, 4, 7, and 8 use the bottom-up approach.

The third question is, "What will drive the search process?" The bottom-up approach is to generate predictions of where to insert chunks by looking at the chunks themselves and determining where in the interlingua structure they might fit in. Strategies 1, 3, 5, and 7 use the bottom-up approach (figure 8.9).

The top-down approach is to look at the interlingua structure, determine what slot is likely to be filled in, and look for a chunk which might fill that slot. Strategies 2, 4, 6, and 8 use the top-down approach (figure 8.10).

The difference between these strategies is primarily in the ordering of hypotheses. But there is also some difference in the breadth of the search space. The bottom-up approach will only generate hypotheses about chunks which it has. And if there is some doubt about what the type of a chunk is, only a finite number of possibilities will be tested, and none of these may match something which can be inserted into one of the available slots. The top-down approach generates its predictions based on what is likely to fit into available slots in the current interlingua structure. It first tries to find a likely filler which matches a chunk that has a definite type, but in the absence of this eventuality, it will assume that a chunk with no specific type is whatever type it guesses can fit

Question: How will constituents be built?

Answer: Try Top-Down.

Available Chunks:

1. ((value be))
2. ((frame *free) (who ((frame *i))) (good-bad +))
3. ((frame *that))
4. ((frame *simple-time) (time-of-day afternoon) (day-of-week Tuesday) (day 9))

Constituents:

1. ((frame *simple-time) (time-of-day afternoon) (day-of-week Tuesday) (day 9))
2. ((frame *free) (who ((frame *i))) (good-bad +))
3. ((frame *i))
4. ((frame *that))
5. ((value be))

Figure 8.8
The second question.

Question: What will drive the search process?

Answer: Try Bottom-Up.

Current Constituent:

((frame *simple-time)
 (time-of-day afternoon)
 (day-of-week Tuesday)
 (day 9)))

Hypothesis:

(frame-slot ((frame-name *free)
(when ((frame *simple-time)
        (time-of-day afternoon)
        (day-of-week Tuesday)
        (day 9)))))

Question: Is Tuesday afternoon the ninth the time of being free in your sentence?

User Response: *Yes.*

New Current Interlingua Structure:

((sentence-type *state)
 (frame *free)
 (when ((frame *simple-time)
        (time-of-day afternoon)
        (day-of-week Tuesday)
        (day 9))))

Figure 8.9
The third question—part 1.

Question: What will drive the search process?
Answer: Try Top-Down.
Current Slot: who
Hypothesis: (frame-slot ((frame-name *free) (who ((frame *i)))))
Question: Is it "I" who is being free in your sentence?
User Response: *Yes.*
New Current Interlingua Structure:
((sentence-type *state)
 (frame *free)
 (who ((frame *i)))
 (when ((frame *simple-time)
        (time-of-day afternoon)
        (day-of-week Tuesday)
        (day 9))))

Figure 8.10
The third question—part 2.

into a slot. And if the user confirms that this slot should be filled with this type, it will learn the mapping between the symbols in that chunk and that type. Learning new words is more likely to occur with the top-down approach than with the bottom-up approach.

The meta-strategy answers these questions, selecting the strategy to employ at a given time. Once a strategy is selected, it continues until it either makes a repair or cannot generate any more questions given the current state of the Dynamic Repair Memory. Also, once the first question is answered, it is never asked again since once the top-level frame is confirmed, it can be depended upon to be correct.

The meta-strategy attempts to answer the first question at the beginning of the search process. If the whole input utterance parses or the parse quality indicated by the parser is good and the top-level frame guessed as most likely by the mutual information nets matches the one chosen by the parser, it assumes it should take the top-down approach. If the parse quality is bad, it assumes it should guess a new top-level frame, but it does not remove the current top-level frame from its list of possible top-level frames. In all other cases, it confirms with the user whether the top-level frame selected by the parser is the correct one and if it is not, then it proceeds through its list of hypotheses until it locates the correct top-level frame.

Currently, the meta-strategy always answers the second question the same way. Preliminary results indicated that in the great majority of cases, the repair module was more effective when it took the top-down approach. It is most often the case that the chunks that are needed can be located within the structures of the chunks returned by the parser without combining them. And even when it is the case that chunks should be combined in order to form a chunk that fits into the current interlingua structure, the same effect can be generated by mapping the top-level structure of the would-be combined chunk onto an available chunk with an uncertain type and then inserting the would-be constituent chunks into this hypothesized chunk later. Preliminary tests indicated that the option of combining chunks only yielded an increase in accuracy in about 1% of the 129 cases tested. Nevertheless, it would be ideal for the meta-strategy to sense when it is likely to be useful to take this approach, no matter how infrequent. This is a direction for future research.

The third question is answered by taking the bottom-up approach early, considering only chunks with a definite type and then using a top-down approach for the duration of the repair process for the current interlingua structure.

The final task of the meta-strategy is for it to decide when to stop asking questions. Currently it does this when there are no open slots or it has asked some arbitrary maximum number of questions. An important direction for future research is to find a better way of doing this. Currently, the repair module asks primarily useful questions (yielding an increase in accuracy) early (within the first 5 or 10 questions) and then proceeds to ask a lot of irrelevant questions. But we have not found an optimal maximum number of questions. If the number of questions is too small, it will not be able to learn some new input patterns and sometimes fails to recover information it would have been able to recover had it been allowed to ask a few more questions. But if the number is too large, it is unnecessarily annoying for the user, particularly in cases where the important information was recovered early in the process.

5.3   User Interaction

User interaction is an essential part of our approach. The ideal in speech-to-speech translation has been direct throughput from input speech to output speech. But this leaves the speaker with no idea of what the system understood from what was said or what is ultimately communicated to the other speaker. This is particularly a problem with flexible parsing techniques where the parser must take some liberties in finding a parse for ill-formed input. An example interaction is displayed in figure 8.11. The interlingua representations for the example sentence before and after repair are displayed in figure 8.12.

The sample interaction in figure 8.11 was collected during system testing when a user unfamiliar with the system was given the task of communicating

SYSTEM: Please enter a sentence (or quit):
USER: I am afraid I will be attending the funeral of my precious canary next week.
SYSTEM: Is your sentence mainly about an interjection?
USER: No.
SYSTEM: Is your sentence mainly about being available?
USER: No.
SYSTEM: Is your sentence mainly about someone being busy?
USER: Yes.
SYSTEM: Is your sentence a short but complete sentence?
USER: No.
SYSTEM: Is your sentence a statement?
USER: Yes.
SYSTEM: Is the next week in focus in your expression of someone being busy?
USER: Yes.
SYSTEM: Is it I who is being busy in your sentence?
USER: Yes.
SYSTEM: Is a class the reason for being busy in your sentence?
USER: No.
SYSTEM: Is being available the reason for being busy in your sentence?
USER: No.

Figure 8.11
Example interaction.

to the system that he would not be available for a meeting the following week. The parser was unable to parse most of his utterance. The parse before repair is displayed in figure 8.12. The portion of his utterance which the parser returned an analysis for completely misses most of the content of the user's utterance. Through a series of yes/no questions, the repair module was able to extract the essential meaning of the user's utterance from the partial parse. The purpose of the first three questions in the sample interaction is for the repair module to determine what the top-level semantic frame of the meaning representation of the sentence should be. With the next two questions the repair module determines the sentence type of the sentence. The last four questions are for determining what the slot fillers for the representation should be. The resulting interlingua representation can be found in figure 8.12.

Because our Hypothesis Generation Module makes hypotheses about local repairs, the questions generated focus on local information in the meaning representation of the sentence. For instance, rather than confirm global meaning

Parse before repair:
((sentence-type *fixed-expression)
(type ((adverb unfortunately)
(frame *adverb)))
(frame *interject))

Paraphrase:
"Unfortunately"

Parse after repair:
((sentence-type *state)
(frame *busy)
(who ((frame *i)))
(topic ((specifier (*multiple* definite next))
(frame *special-time)
(name week)))))

Paraphrase:
"The next week I don't have time."

Figure 8.12
Interlingua structures for example before and after repair.

representations as in , "Did you mean to say X?," it confirms local information as in, "Is two o'clock the time of being busy in your sentence?," which confirms that the representation for "two o'clock" should be inserted into the *when* slot in the *busy frame. Because the repair module generates local repair hypotheses, with each decision building upon the result of the last successful hypothesis, through trial and error it is forced to ask a large number of very tedious questions. An important current direction of research is exploring how to minimize this burden on the user while maximizing the information the repair module can extract from the user's utterances through the use of a genetic programming approach to maximize the mutual information over a single global repair hypothesis made up of a combination of local repair hypotheses.

6 Quantitative Evaluation

The repair module was tested on two corpora with 129 sentences each. One corpus contains 129 transcribed sentences from spontaneous scheduling dialogues as described above. The other corpus contains the output from the speech recognizer from reading the transcribed sentences. So it contains all of the difficulties of the transcribed corpus in addition to speech-recognition errors. The performance of the repair module was compared with a baseline process on an additional corpus of 113 sentences. These results indicate that the performance of the repair module improves as the number of questions increases, that its performance generalizes to different data sets, and that the meta-strategy consistently achieves better performance than any of the single strategies as well as the baseline comparison process.

The repair module was evaluated automatically with no human intervention whatever. Prior to the evaluation, a human coder hand-coded ideal interlingua representations for each of the 129 sentences. The human-computer interaction component of the repair module was simulated by having the computer match each proposed repair against the ideal interlingua structure for the corresponding sentence to test whether it would make the current "in-progress" version of the interlingua representation internal to the repair module more like the ideal one. Each of these tests counted as one question. If the match indicated that the proposed repair was a good one, a "yes" answer was assumed, otherwise a "no" answer was assumed. If the answer was "yes," the repair module made the hypothesized repair. After each question, the possibly updated internal interlingua representation was matched with the ideal one to calculate a point value. The matching process was carried out recursively, first comparing the top-level frame, and if it was the same for each slot, comparing the fillers in the ideal structure with the corresponding ones in the internal structure. For each matching frame or atom, one point was assigned. The total possible was computed by counting the total number of frames and atoms in the ideal representation. From this, a percentage correct could be calculated at each stage of the repair process to track the improvement of the quality of the internal representation per question asked.

Figure 8.13 displays the relative performance of the eight strategies compared with the meta-strategy on speech data. Figure 8.14 displays the relative performance of the strategies on the transcribed data. Note that the meta-strategy consistently achieves a better performance than any of the single strategies and that its performance improves as the number of questions allowed increases.

Given a maximum of 10 questions to ask the user, the repair module can raise the accuracy of the parser from 52% to 64% on speech data and from 68% to 78% on transcribed data. Given a maximum of 25 questions, it can raise the accuracy to 72% on speech data and 86% on transcribed data.

The baseline for comparison was a process consisting of building the correct interlingua structure from a Huffman-coded version of the interlingua specification where each node in the Huffman tree counted as one question. A Huffman tree was constructed for each type in the interlingua specification. The comparison process began by trying to guess the top-level semantic frame by traversing the Huffman tree for top-level frames. It then continued the process

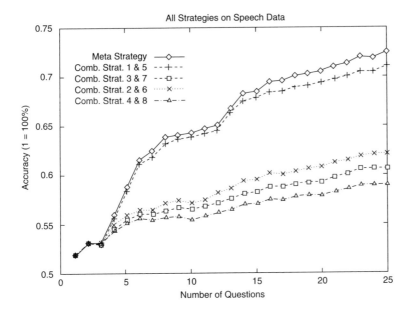

Figure 8.13
Results from all strategies on speech data.

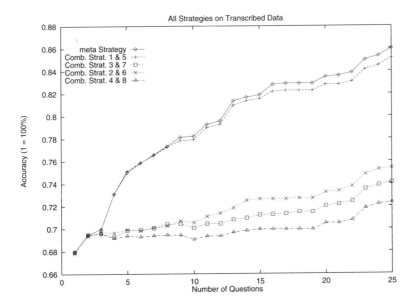

Figure 8.14
Results from all strategies on transcribed data.

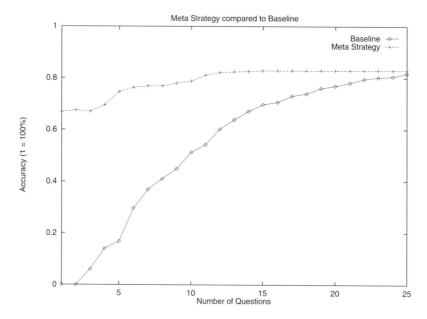

Figure 8.15
Results from meta-strategy compared with baseline.

recursively constructing fillers for each of the slots using the Huffman tree for
the type corresponding to the slot. This process corresponds to an extreme version of the repair process not using any information from the parser whatever.
The results of comparing the meta-strategy with the comparison process on the
additional data set can be found in figure 8.15. Note that the meta-strategy is
consistently better than the comparison process.

7   Qualitative Evaluation

The repair module's ability to make repairs of various sorts is determined by
two parameters which guide the search process. The first is the maximum number of questions it is allowed to ask, and the second is what is called the bandwidth. Bandwidth is used in two different ways in the current implementation
of the repair module. It specifies how long the list of likely types will be
assigned to a chunk with an uncertain type and how many potential slots will
be considered when a top-down approach is selected for driving the search
process. This parameter is set for practical reasons so that the repair module
will spend the majority of its time considering hypotheses that are truly likely.

If the maximum number of questions were infinite, it would not be important to have such a parameter. In practice, with a small finite number of questions, it is important. It forces the repair module to sample a larger area within its search space more shallowly instead of looking at a very small area in depth. In the future, bandwidth and maximum number of questions will be replaced with a confidence model.

The problem with setting a bandwidth is that it makes certain potential repairs impossible and affects the repair module's ability to learn. If the correct hypothesis in a particular case is extremely unlikely according to the statistical model, it will not most likely be ranked within the bandwidth, so it will never be considered. The maximum number of questions is similar. In some cases, where the correct hypothesis is extremely unlikely, the repair module will not be able to hone in on it within its maximum number of questions. In the case that the repair module is faced with the task of mapping new words onto a less frequently encountered concept, if it never manages to get to the correct hypotheses within its maximum number of questions, it will not be able to learn that mapping.

With an infinite bandwidth and infinite number of questions, the repair module would have the ability to make any repair. This is intuitive because even with no information from the parse, by cycling through the possible top-level frames and sentence types, it would eventually arrive at the correct combination. From there it knows from the interlingua specification what the possible fillers for each of the slots are, and by cycling through all of those possibilities it would eventually arrive at the correct interpretation.

It is not practical to allow the repair module to operate this way, however. First of all, it is much more practical to make use of information from the parse where it is available (see figure 8.15). In some cases, this means relying upon the parser to produce reliable results. If the repair module confirmed every piece of information in the feature-structure returned by the parser, it would ask far too many useless questions. On the other hand, if it took an all-or-nothing approach, it might throw out potentially useful portions of the analysis from the parser. Currently, it only checks to see if the top-level semantic frame returned by the parser is correct. If it is, it keeps the whole partial analysis returned by the parser; otherwise it starts from scratch, using portions of the parser's partial analysis wherever possible. If it keeps the whole partial analysis, however, it may retain portions of it which are not correct. With a more reliable confidence model, this compromise would not be necessary.

One additional shortcut we have taken is not to allow the repair module to postulate date representations which the parser is not able to identify as date material. This is because there is no such thing as a "most likely date," so it is unclear how to build a statistical model which could make useful predictions about date fillers outside of context, especially since there are an infinite number of possible date representations.

8 Conclusions and Current Directions

This chapter describes an approach to interactive repair of fragmented parses in the context of a speech-to-speech translation project of significant scale. It makes it possible to use symbolic knowledge sources to the extent that they are available and uses statistical knowledge to fill in the gaps. This gives it the ability to keep the preciseness of symbolic approaches wherever possible as well as the robustness of statistical approaches wherever symbolic knowledge sources are not available. It is a general approach which applies regardless of how degraded the input is, even if the sentence completely fails to parse.

The primary weakness of this approach is that it relies too heavily on user interaction. One goal of current research is to reduce this burden on the user. Current directions include exploring a genetic programming technique for generating global repair hypotheses, eliminating the need for many tedious questions such as the ones described in this chapter, as well as exploring the use of discourse and domain knowledge for the purpose of eliminating hypotheses that do not make sense.

Acknowledgments

C.P.R. offers special thanks to her co-author Alex Waibel for advising her master's research and also to her two other master's committee members, Lori Levin and David Evans, for making helpful contributions.

The research described in this chapter was sponsored by the Department of Naval Research, grant #N00014-93-1-0806. The ideas described here do not necessarily reflect the position or policy of the government, and no official endorsement should be inferred.

References

J. G. Carbonell and P. J. Hayes. Recovery strategies for parsing extragrammatical language. Technical Report 84-87, School of Computer Science, Carnegie Mellon University, Pittsburgh, 1984.

J. R. Hobbs, D. E. Appelt, and J. Bear. Robust processing of real-world natural-language texts. Trent, Italy, 1992. Third Conference on Applied NLP.

A. Lavie and M. Tomita. GLR*—an efficient noise-skipping parsing algorithm. Presented at 3rd International Workshop on Parsing Technologies, 1993. Tilburg, The Netherlands.

J. F. Lehman. *Self-Extending Natural Language Interfaces.* Ph.D. thesis, School of Computer Science, Carnegie Mellon University, Pittsburg, 1989.

D. McDonald. The interplay of syntactic and semantic node labels in partial parsing. Presented at 3rd International Workshop on Parsing Technologies, 1993.

M. Woszcyna, N. Coccaro, A. Eisele, A. Lavie, A. McNair, T. Polzin, I. Rogina, C. P. Rosé, T. Sloboda, M. Tomita, J. Tsutsumi, N. Waibel, A. Waibel, and W. Ward. Recent advances in JANUS: A speech translation system. ARPA Human Language Technology Workshop, 1993. Plainsboro, New Jersey.

Contributors

Steven Abney
University of Tübingen
Tübingen, Germany

Hiyan Alshawi
AT&T Bell Laboratories
Murray Hill, New Jersey

Robin Clark
University of Pennsylvania
Philadelphia, Pennsylvania

Béatrice Daille
TALANA, University of Paris
Paris, France

Vasileios Hatzivassiloglou
Columbia University
New York, New York

Shyam Kapur
James Cook University
of North Queensland
Townsville, Australia

Mitchell P. Marcus
University of Pennsylvania
Philadelphia, Pennsylvania

Patti Price
SRI International
Menlo Park, California

Lance A. Ramshaw
University of Pennsylvania
Philadelphia, Pennsylvania
Bowdoin College
Brunswick, Maine

Carolyn Penstein Rosé
Carnegie Mellon University
Pittsburgh, Pennsylvania

Alex H. Waibel
Carnegie Mellon University
Pittsburgh, Pennsylvania

Index